REDEFINE

A COLLECTION OF FEMALE FOUNDERS ON RISING & REDEFINING THEIR SUCCESS

ALLISON RAMSEY   MEGAN COREY   IIYSE CRAFT

MINDY GREEN   ELIANE LEPINE   OXANA ROMANYUK

LITA VALLIS   LAURA WALL   JENNA ZANTUA

Published in the United States through Amazon

 Kindle Direct Publishing www.amazon.com

Kindle Direct Publishing are

Registered trademarks of Amazon.

Library of Congress Cataloging-In-Publication

Data is available upon request.

ISBN

Ebook ISBN

PRINTED IN THE UNITED STATES OF AMERICA

Book Design by Empire Life, LLC

Book Formatting by Michelle Morrow www.chellreads.com

First Edition

This is for our legacy,

for those humans coming into their voice,

for my family, for our families and loved ones,

for all the female founders.

FOREWORD

I was doing deep breathing exercises on the floor on my back when the idea came to me. The idea came in clear, "Publish a book with a group of women, give them your platform for promoting their businesses and giving them more of a voice, to have their stories heard."

After this idea came to me I had a day full of connection calls with amazing ladies. The first call I had after this, I mentioned to her about writing a book, my first one. She started telling me about a few friends of hers publishing collaborative books, as well. I asked her about how much she felt the fee needed to be published in the book. She was my first author to join the book for us to collaborate together, on that call.

I started to connect stronger every day with my intention to bring female founder voices to the forefront. Understanding how their voices will change, inspire and catapult other women's lives. My highest intention is to have people read these stories and have something stand out for them to inspire or change their lives for the better.

We all had pivoting moments we are sharing here vulnerability to give you the keys to pivot or catapult your success. Often these moments we are sharing were times we were not understanding how to get up, move forward, crying on the bathroom floor, until we did understand the beauty in our growth and newly bridged mindsets.

Thankful for my mom displaying great financial planning skills. Grateful to my dad for displaying hard work and a sound work ethic. Proud of my brother and thankful for his presence in my life.

From humble beginnings to massive and continued success. For the authors here, we have all come into our success and continue to rise together and REDEFINE our success for the best life possible.

REDEFINE

ALLISON RAMSEY

Whenever I requested something outside of my parents' budget, it was a knee jerk reaction to hear this from their lips. My parents often told me the saying, "Money doesn't grow on trees," more times than I can recount growing up. There was nothing malicious about it, it was part of our generational programming and patterns. They wanted to instill in my brother and me how we had to work hard for our money, and the value of money.

My mom is one of the best financial planners I know. She has been actively planning the family's money for most of my life growing up. She was an officer in a ladies' investment group as well, for a long time. I would often tag along with her and converse with the ladies at the local ladies investment group luncheons. At that time, I mostly found these luncheons to be boring, actually eye dropping almost sleeping, not quite understanding the value proposition in the benefits of letting our money compound through investing, at the time.

MONEY TALKS

There was not a lot of talk about making money with ease in our immediate family or extended family. The central theme of making money was often centered around 'suffering'. A common thread throughout my family is how one needed to go without and suffer a great deal to bring in a lot of money, or any money at all. This theory has been extended to over-working and coming to sheer burnout, otherwise, the direct message you would be told in one way or another is, *you could still do more and you are not done yet!*

Through immense processing of my over-achievement and intense drive, I often asked myself: *Is there more here I could do here? How late can I stay up working on projects before I pass out from needing sleep? How many more hours do I need to practice basketball to never have the coach question whether to start me in the games or not? How can I make the highest grade here? How can I outwork everyone in the office? How many clients are we capable of taking on, right now? Why did that person receive that, did they even work very much for it?* To be clear for a lot of my life, I would not stop until I proved myself to be the best in my area. For me, I started to notice, this could also resemble suffering, sacrifice, and not understanding when I was about to reach pure burning out. I was not able to tap into the flowing, effortless, or easier way of doing *anything*. I hardly believed in breaks and aimed to finish everything as quickly and as efficiently as possible, sometimes giving orders to my colleagues to speed up, to do more, or to change their course to be more efficient, and rarely listened to them if they offered an easier way to do something.

It was not only my programming of learning to suffer, sacrifice, and have grit beyond measure. You see, I had been born with a pure emboldened fierce fire inside of me that kept pushing me regardless of how I felt or if it felt like sacrificing. I have kept a journal of inspiring quotes for at least fifteen years, and one of them I used to live by was, *"I won't stop fighting until the gorilla of life gets tired."* As one can imagine, my inner strength of character, grit, attitude, and relentlessness brought me into rooms where I never imagined I would be. However, it also led to sheer burnout, sometimes, sleeping for days after a semester of college finished and I had the A's to prove to myself and the world. Yet after a project or college semester came to a close, I often slept for days on end, unable to barely talk, and recuperated. *At what point could I rest intermittently without feeling guilty, without feeling I needed to prove myself to the world? At what point could I say, I've done everything I can, go to sleep, save my resources, and replenish them for the next day?* These questions eventually become answered after many life lessons, learnings, personal growth, crying sessions on the floor barely able to get up, and unwinding of taught philosophies. I started to create, design, blueprint, and compose my collection of philosophies on life and how I desired to live my life!

The unintentional messaging was communicated to members of my family through actions, stories, and direct advice of, *'you get to feel deserving of money once you have suffered adequately.'* There has been a long line of suffering related to making money within my family for generations. On various occasions, my parents did not see eye to eye about how money was to be spent within the family. Without blame, this created tension which I unconsciously internalized about money and worked through later in life.

Sometimes my dad will buy something and whisper to me, as he was buying it, "Don't tell your mom."

My mom taught me a lot of great lessons about saving money and stretching every dollar as thin as possible. I'm greatly enamored with myself when I find a good deal and love to save money. Although, still quite a feat for me, I've learned to release what I cannot control related to money and trusting the process of how it comes back. I came to resonate with the phrase: *In trusting the process of how everything always works out for the best.* I have learned how money is a continuous flow: I focus on making choices where I feel great about giving it and then also focus on being a money magnet as it flows back in.

THE DOLLAR MENU

While growing up, my mom always had her coupon holder in her purse. When we were out and about, and my brother and I were hungry, she would pull out her coupon holder and go through them. We would get choices from the coupons: *$1 Quarter Pounder, $1 Big Mac, or Arby's buy one sandwich and get one free.* We had to choose one of the coupons, and all three of us had to agree on the choice. I often debated with my brother about the choice, up until the point where my mom would need to make the final choice. Often, I *just did not eat* because I did not want fast food. Usually, this was because fast food hurt my stomach, I was avoiding inevitable pain. At the time, I would rather choose hunger pains over stomach pains from the food I ate.

My stomach hurt quite frequently, enough for my mom to take me to the doctor and ask him why my stomach was hurting all the time. After extensive tests, the doctor could not find anything wrong with me. Often he prescribed medicines to offer soothing feelings for my constant stomach ache and other medicines for coughs, ear infections, or allergies. My mom gave me some of the medicines, which commonly caused me to projectile vomit, vomit all day, have back spasms, and other extremely unpleasant side effects. I became traumatized by these experiences from having allergic reactions to medications. She was doing her best, and my other sibling did not have these reactions to the medications. At some point, my mom took me back to the doctor and told him I was allergic to almost every medication he had prescribed. I remember I despised the doctors waiting room and did not feel I was truly sick to go there, since I was often complaining about my aches and allergic reactions. We needed to go to see him again to inquire about our options in finding a solution to my consistent repulsiveness and avoidance of medications.

My mom said to the doctor, "What else can we do?"

He shrugged his shoulders and said, "Well maybe she'll grow out of it."

I became the kid who would run for her life when being given medicine. I'd mischievously run and hide, and became super sneaky with getting out of taking the medicine. She'd put the medicine in ham and cheese and somehow I'd still sniff it out. She'd also put it in my drinks and I'd find out refusing to consume it. In retrospect, I understand and give grace to myself, this was all part of my blueprint and learning about my money mindset and my body. Even as a child, I knew things were out of alignment, and eating food based on coupon choices every time we got to dine out, was making me sick. I was meant to transform my parents' eating habits, and eventually, transform my own as well. They now eat healthy, organic food, and hardly ever drink sodas.

THE BIG GULP

When I was growing up my mom would sometimes stop by the gas station to refill her giant Dr. Pepper soda cup, called a BIG GULP. It didn't fit in the cupholder. I would need to hold it for her while she was driving. You only bought the cup once, and the refills were 50 cents. On occasion, she'd get me a candy bar too, and I was only allowed to eat a few bites, to not ruin my next meal, or give me a sugar high. Every time she got the giant soda refilled I'd say things to her, gently such as: *Mom you know this has a lot of sugar right? Mom, in science class we learned that there's an acid in sodas that dissolves stomach linings and our teeth, it can even dissolve a penny.*

Mom do you need this much, this cup is pretty big. Every time met with: *Oh, stop it!* I report back that my parents do not drink soda anymore, for a long time.

BANKRUPTCY

As I grew older my money journey was riddled with mishaps, completely by my design. There was much to unlearn and unwind. Towards the end of my mishaps, I started to create new patterns for myself, before this I dove into my first company headfirst without knowing anything about business, or how to maintain a successful empire. I had a lot to learn about business, sales, maintaining financials, and more. I became a mom and single mom in my early 20's, then I started my first business, and my daughter grew up seeing me working two to three jobs simultaneously. She attended many business meetings, client meetings, and private sessions along with her iPad on tow or me giving her my phone to watch YouTube.

After becoming bankrupt from over-investing into my first company, without sustaining the clients I needed to pay my bills and order inventory. I rightfully and temporarily gave up on being my own boss. I desperately needed a break, but still felt I was meant to be a successful business owner. I had lost hope in, and went to work full time in education, and made my business a side project. I pursued education because I was able to have more time off with my daughter while she was little. Eventually, when she was older I went full time into technology, software, and full time in my business again. In 2009, after finishing my Master's in Science (M.S.), and gaining my

Texas teaching certification, I had a great (yet scary in retrospect) opportunity to live in Turkey with my daughter. The teaching job paid for our new two-story luxury townhouse, her private international school, our health insurance, and then I was paid on top of this.

For the first time in my life, I realized how it felt to have all of my financial needs met. And I had free time with my daughter to explore Istanbul. Sadly, I quickly understood I had handed over control of my life, my working hours, and home to my employer. My employer let their family members visiting Istanbul stay at our house, without asking. I felt extraordinarily uncomfortable with having strangers in our house, especially with a toddler. Almost every time there would be guests at our house, I would take my daughter and go stay with friends. I moved us out and changed jobs after the final straw broke the camel's back, they told me they were not going to pay me in the summer months and did not refrain from having guests when my family was visiting me.

It was a rough new beginning moving across the city of Istanbul to the Asian side from the European side with a toddler. There were many new items to set up at our new apartment, however, I felt I could probably do *just about anything* since I had succeeded at renting an apartment, moving across the city, and finding a new job with a toddler in a foreign country.

FOUNDER AND MOM ENTREPRENEUR

My daughter learned from an early age how to behave in business meetings. When we lived in Turkey, I would often have my consultations in the same restaurants. Since I did not have any family in Turkey, or close friends living near me, I'd need to take her with me. The restaurant servers knew me and how I was running my business and consultations from their patio area. I'd usually be doing English tutoring lessons for two hundred lire an hour, or I'd be doing natural medicine consultations for two hundred and fifty lire an hour. They often would not charge my food and only charge my client, and also would give my daughter complimentary food. The restaurant staff knew her favorite foods and were always smiling and delighted to see her. She was allowed to run around the restaurant, but still, it was challenging because I found my attention diverted from my client towards making sure my baby was safe when she sometimes went out of eyesight. I found peace of mind in knowing my daughter was happy and comfortable and in knowing the restaurant staff. I'm thankful for how the Turkish culture is kid-friendly and respectful, supportive, and welcoming towards families and mothers.

I found another teaching job, higher-paying, and moved us across the city, also I was still doing my private lessons and consultations for clients. There were a lot of complications with the new job and the paperwork needed. My daughter and I lived separately from each other for a few months. I cried every day while she and I were part, in that time I saved a lot of money in the next months and decided for us to fully move back to the USA for more job opportunities and smoother sailing. There were a lot of loose ends to tie up in Istanbul and move our lives back to the USA. One of the huge processes I went through before leaving Istanbul is I declared bankruptcy in the USA. The bankruptcy damaged my credit for five to seven years after declaring it. It also put a horrible taste in my mouth for my ability to manage money and a business. *The bankruptcy shook my world.* When I moved back to the USA, we needed to live with my parents to build my credit for at least six months, to even be able to rent an apartment. I needed a car right away when moving back to Texas because as I write this, there is little public transportation in Texas. I had to pay for the used car in cash, as I was unable to take out a loan.

For a lot of years, I did not tell people about the bankruptcy because it took a few years to forgive myself. I was deeply afraid they would judge me because I was judging myself every day about it. In the second year of being back in the USA, I started a second business with another software developer. I started to gain confidence in running my own business again, yet the other co-founder and I parted ways after two years in business. I deeply learned again to ask for support. One of the breaking points of my second co-founded company was he was unable to ask for support. From my perspective, it prevented our company from reaching its full potential. It was utterly painful to sit by as I witnessed what felt like a huge birth in launching, flying, and then crashing and burning. Many days I will ask the other co-founder if he will ask for support, or research how he and I would be better apt to scale our company.

I was met with him stating to me: *I cannot help it if you are stupid and have the desire to think stupidly, unlike me, I know how to research on my own. You and I just need to research, code, and think more.* In other words, he felt, in no uncertain terms, asking for help was *stupid.* When he and I decided to put the company on the back burner, I was devastated and desired to continue the legacy of being my own boss and leaving a company and legacy for my child. At one point I asked him to have access to some parts of the code he had built and he denied me admin access to it. Without the combination of my code and his code, there was no web application I could run. Another option was to rebuild all the code myself, and this was unlikely to happen with a young child and a full-time job. Eventually, I experienced the company parishing by default of peacefully needing to let it go. What co-founding my second company did guide me on was a newfound confidence in coding, in launching, and mapping out a successful company. There was some success in my second co-founded company, yet the plateau happened when he and I did not seek support outside our present knowledge base. There was a lack of sales, marketing, or business experience at the time. He and I were in desperate need of a business, sales, or marketing team or mentors to tell us our blind spots. I did not know it then, yet crying every day for at least one year over the loss of this company, witnessing this company slowly perishing, brought new knowingness and wisdom. Sometimes people ask me if he and I sold the company, I want to answer, yes, yet sadly it never reached its full-scale potential to be viable for selling. In learning from my previous company, as a software developer and coder myself, it is always best to have access to all the code on a system. In access, I mean full rights to all systems, contracts with clauses about what will happen with the dissolving of the company if it were to come to this, and full admin access to the code.

Also, it is best to have a team of people who see your blind spots, who have unique expertise to yours, and delegate while scaling. As the saying goes, "We don't know what we don't know". However, my intentions of fully launching and scaling my second company, a tech company catapulting and promoting natural health practitioners were pure. When I look back I was unaware of a lot of mindset tools and strategies I now have and am continuing to learn. At this point in my life, I have a team of support, mentors, loved ones, journaling, daily habits, and a lot more self-love plus self-acceptance. I was still pushing and forcing myself to succeed in my second company, as opposed to having a balance in flowing and pushing. Also, I have no regrets because there was nothing more I could have said to the co-founder to convince him to ask for support or motivate him to understand the need for outside support. I was also forgiving myself in my second company about having a less than the desired outcome in my first company with filing for bankruptcy. As I was forgiving myself, I deferred a lot of the business decisions and financial choices to my co-founder because I built confidence. Over time, and after some self-forgiveness I became more secure in my abilities to fully lead a company again and financially felt secure and abundant.

I was brought successful people in my path who shared with me about them having their bankruptcy (ies) too. I started to see it was more common in successful business owners than most realize. How most founders have had at least one bankruptcy in one of their earlier businesses.

Still, I was hesitant to start another company, my third company, hence I buried myself in working for others in software and tech roles. I love being in technology and am grateful to continue my path in data analytics, software development, artificial intelligence, and everything tech. I was the employee who did everything possible for the company I was at unless it affected being there for my daughter. I always wanted her to feel my presence and found it important to spend as much time with her as possible outside of work.

THE TRAIN IS MINE

This story was buried deep in my subconscious until a conversation brought it to the surface. I asked a lot of questions growing up and have always possessed an insatiable curiosity. When I was around three years old my mom put me in a preschool a few days a week. Immediately my new best friend, Michelle, and I found each other. My good friend, Michelle, had a full-sized real train on the bottom floor of her three-story house. A train *just* for her, our size to ride. I rode it when I was at her house. When I came home from her house, I told my mom about this experience.

My mom said to me, "You'll never be going there again, and don't invite her over."

I said, "I don't understand, I had fun, why can't I go there or why can't I have my friend come over?"

She said, "I don't see any reason why a three-year-old needs a full-size train in her house and I don't want you thinking you need that."

I said, "I don't think I need that. I did enjoy riding it though. I don't understand. She's still my best friend!"

I came to believe money heightens more of who we are, for example, if we are already generous, then we will be more generous with money as we have more. I believe money does not make people one way or another, it was already who they were that is expressed when more power or more money is given to them.

I decided I was coming for the whole train a few years ago.

DEFINING SUFFERING AND FINDING BALANCE

One of the interesting topics in life is how we all have different philosophies about what suffering means to us. Some examples of how I define suffering could be saying yes to everything, having poor boundaries, not planning out our finances, and running everywhere at once with no direction or structure. The way to conquer suffering for me is to guide others in having a strong voice, and in myself expressing and having a positive voice, impact, and influence on my environment. I feel this is part of living in abundance also one of the main purposes of my why in publishing this book series. This book is to give other women the platform to have their voices and stories heard, and indirectly this excels can lead to their businesses scaling with this exposure.

Anytime I suffered in my life I am sure I was not analyzing, or present in the moment about how I was suffering. Most likely I was reacting and thinking I was doing my best at the moment. Neither did my parents or grandparents, or any family thinks they were suffering when living their lives. I have come to believe much of how we respond, what we do, and how we act are steaming from childhood traumas and learned patterns.

Sometimes being in a victim mindset allows us to suffer even more. I feel when we ask ourselves such questions as below, these lead us into an even deeper victim mindset,

"Why does this always happen to me?"

"Why me?"

"Why are they rich and I am not?"

"Do I need that?"

"Why does no one ever seem to be there for me?"

"Why do I feel alone?"

"Why doesn't anyone ever help me?"

"Why does he/she have that car, that house, those kid(s), or that husband/wife and I don't?"

"Why does it feel like I'm just unlucky?"

Changing these questions and altering them to new questions or phrases, gives us a new lease on life,

"Why not me?"

"Of course."

"Money always flows in for me."

"I'm taken care of."

"I'm supported."

"Good things always happen for me, and to me."

"Right now, if I have yet to see the outcome I want, I'll be patient because I know for sure the best outcoming is coming."

"Everything always works out for me."

"I am wise, and I am abundant."

"I have all the support I need."

"People, friends, and family want to be there for me, sometimes I just need to ask."

"I can always speak up and ask for what I desire."

"I know what I want."

"I like indulging in my self-care and self-love."

"I can easily receive when I desire to."

"I can easily say no when I feel called too."

I am unsure if you have come to your philosophy around what suffering feels like and means to you. I have started the journey and am coming to understand what it takes for me to feel whole, happy, abundant, and affluent. It feels powerful to come to our boundaries around suffering. I have worked multiple jobs for as long as I can remember. As I write this I technically have 3 roles. I love it all. I am the founder of Empire Life, a University Professor, and a Mom. Some might view this as I work a lot since I love all of these and none of them felt much like work. The goal is to find something you are passionate about and it will feel less like work. I'm used to putting in a lot of hours, and with doing something I love the hours do usually fly by. With all that fire, determination, and drive I have, it's healthy for it to be directed towards projects for the greater good. I'm always thinking of new structures, strategies, new teammates to train to lessen my load, and can at this time ask comfortably for support.

GRANDPA ADVENTURES

When I was growing up my Grandpa worked long hours of physical labor. My Grandpa will wake me up at 5:30 am when I stayed with them in the summer to go to work with him. I was too young to stay home and if I did stay home there was nothing to do but watch TV. I was an extremely energetic passionate child, I preferred ultimately to go be with my Grandpa. However, the huge grey work van my Grandpa was driving, only had an AM radio and no air conditioning.

With temperatures averaging 40 to 50 Celsius and 100 to 105 Fahrenheit during most Texas summer days, we were sweating non-stop. The only break from the heat was walking into super air-conditioned stores to deliver snacks in big boxes. We will carry boxes to big grocery stores, gas stations, and college campus stores, then unload all the boxes contents onto the shelves in a beautiful display. We did this from 6 am to 6 pm every day, eating a snack for lunch on the way to the next store. Then my Grandpa would usually take me to get a coke and some candy afterward before dinner. I was not allowed to complain about the air conditioning or the AM radio. It was incredible how my body quickly assimilated to the heat, AM radio, waking up early, and physical labor.

My Grandpa was a hard worker and did everything he felt he could do for his family. My father also is an extremely hard worker, and usually was always working two to three jobs. As I write this my father still works two jobs and is retired from a third job. The ability and determination to work hard are in my blood. Neither of my grandparents had a college degree, they were happy to have finished high school. My Grandma did not finish high school before having her first child, my mom. They both encouraged their four kids to go to college, and all four kids graduated from college with an undergraduate degree. They desired less suffering for future generations by encouraging them to go to college to have a better life. My parents also encouraged my brother and me to go to college. My brother and I also both have Master's degrees. My Grandma and Grandpa grew up seeing the remnants of the Great Depression and how this affected their parents. They were raised in seeing food rationed and there often was not enough food for the day for families to eat. This led my Grandma to ration food herself even in her adulthood. My mom shared with me that my Grandma when my mom was growing up, would save small tablespoons of leftovers from their family in little dishes.

When I'd stay there with them, my Grandparents were easily angered with me when we'd go out to eat at a buffet because I'd often leave pieces of food on my plate. I did not quite comprehend their anger because at a buffet or any restaurant I'd go-to for the first time I was unsure if I'd like the food or not. They would explain to me to get only a little food on my plate instead of too much to waste.

My Grandpa would say, in a dominant, definitive, and disciplined tone, "Your eyes are bigger than your stomach!"

Having a stealthy work ethic, which my grandparents, and parents demonstrated to me, is an invaluable life lesson. This life lesson has been passed down to me and other family members. When we combine our intelligence, hard work, and gifts this can make the world our oyster. Sheer grit is something I have always had a lot of too, and this can also get people far. In my opinion, learning how to work hard is one of the sheer ways to start to understand the true value of money, appreciate it, and give gratitude to it. I started working my first job at fifteen years old. I was often working multiple jobs before graduating from high school, this showed me a lot about money! Often jobs I had in high school and college were with people who were a lot older than me, they planned to stay in those jobs for a long time. This taught me and allowed me to observe multiple ways people view money and unique money mindset perspectives. I started asking myself: *What did I want for my financial future?* I also had a long road ahead of learning financial planning strategies and flowing into money.

I WANT THE WHOLE PIECE OF GUM

I understand temporarily going without eating out to save more money, continuously budgeting, and always financial planning is needed and imperative on our path to success and in scaling our businesses. What I do not agree with when I was growing up were the extremes within these philosophies around suffering, sacrificing, and going without. For a lot of my life, I was still finding my philosophy about money and how I wanted to live my life. When I was a little older, about ten years old, my mom went back to work. I needed to go to her friend's house after school sometimes until my parents got home. I'd walk to her friend's house with her friend's daughter and son. To state my mom's friend was a stickler for rules, was an understatement, it seemed she had rules for everything!

As a child who questioned everything, her friend did not like it much when I would question her multitude of rules. One time while my mom's friend and I were standing in her kitchen, I looked up and saw some delicious bubblicious gum. There was a whole package of 30 cent gum and it was too high for me to reach.

I looked at my mom's friend and asked her, "Can I have a piece of gum?"

She scowled at me, huffed as she made her way past me in the kitchen, and forcefully pulled down the whole package of gum. Then she grabbed a butter knife and cut the gum into three pieces on a cutting board. As she started to hand me the tiny one-third of the piece of gum, my mouth dropped open.

I said, "Why did you do that, how can I enjoy the gum with this little piece you're giving me. How can I even feel the gum in my mouth?"

She looked perplexed, raised her voice, and said, "You eat the whole piece of gum? Why do you think you need the whole piece of gum? That's not what we do at our house, we save the gum for when we want some later."

I said, "Why would I want anything different than the whole piece of gum? I can barely taste what you gave me."

She said, "Well too bad, that's how we do it here!"

That night my determination came alive, as I was spending the night when the story above happened, after everyone went to bed I sprung into action. I remember waking up with an idea about figuring out a way to get a whole piece of that gum and enjoying it fully. I tip-toed into the kitchen as quietly as possible, picked up a wood kitchen stool, put it by the counter, climbed on the counter from the stool, and took the package of gum down from the hanging wood basket. Then I sat down on the counter, in the dark, cross-legged, unwrapped a whole piece of gum, put it in my mouth, and experienced pure heaven on earth! I tip-toed back to the room and slept well that night.

A new metaphor was made in my life of enjoying the whole piece of gum, as comparing the gum to life itself: *Enjoy the whole piece, take it in, be grateful for it, and relish in it.*

EXTREMES

From my experience sometimes we go from one extreme to the other before understanding and finding a middle way or a balance. In my own life, I felt I went from thinking money was not needed to have a great life to feeling ok with being coined materialistic. At this point, I fully accept my need, desire, and love of money. Plus providing for myself and my loved ones, and working hard to save money, and put in the time with integrity and grit in my work gives me great gratitude for the money I make.

When I was in my early 20's I lived in several different countries and was working three different jobs. Even then I somehow always met wildly wealthy people, who were desiring to befriend me, pass on knowledge, and wisdom to me. Here I was, thinking, it was ok to live in a small studio apartment in Paris in a sub-par district, and it was alright to walk into stores and feel as if I was unable to buy what I desired, somehow I had convinced myself I did not need much.

I went to the extent to tell my mom once, "I don't need much, I can survive with very little money."

The keyword here is, *survive,* at some point, I transformed this into embodying and living in my desire to *thrive* and live beyond my wildest dreams.

My mom told me in response to this in no uncertain terms, "No! You are materialistic, whether you want to admit it or not."

Wow, this statement struck home and hit a sensitive spot inside me, a spot I was not ready to admit yet at that time. I was and am probably materialistic, and am ok with this. Also, I no longer view the word *materialistic* negatively. I'm happy to be comfortable and make the lives of my loved ones better in any way I can.

FROM SUFFERING TO THRIVING

My mom said to me once, about having a lot of money saved, "You gotta have old shoes for a while and be ok paying 20 dollars or less for your shoes while you build your wealth."

This story can be translated to, *doing whatever it takes*, to succeed. While there is truth in this, there is also a lot of suffering in between the truth. However, this philosophy I was raised in, could lead me to believe suffering is non-optional. Such as *having inexpensive shoes, and eating inexpensive food, to succeed, one must suffer to succeed.* I was unconsciously fueling this philosophy until I felt I came to my philosophy of *more of a middle way in my work ethic and a healthy money mindset.*

I had and have great examples of working ourselves hard, sometimes until sheer burnout. I am a believer in learning, growing, and seeking out books, mentors, and support in areas of needed improvement. The goal is to maximize our gifts and efforts in the most efficient way possible.

Growing up in a rough neighborhood I did see entrepreneurs around me, such as: *meth-producing drug labs, prostitution houses, drug dealers, and burglar rings.* These roles and *businesses* do take significant planning, organization, and execution of the goal they aim to meet. I heard often from people around me growing up, regarding others' wealth, when they'd see a *wealthy* person, say, *Oh will you look at that spoiled brat, I bet someone gave that to them. Or they don't deserve that, someone needs to show them.* I often found these messages to be repulsive and did not resonate with these philosophies. As I learned more about abundance, saying or hearing these types of phrases felt extremely out of alignment for me. When altering phrases to be more in alignment with what I wanted and desired for my life and money mindset, at first the new phrases felt a bit foreign because I was used to people looking down on others who *had* money. When desiring to attract and bring in big amounts of money I needed to exile these types of phrases and shift them into: *Wow, I love their car, they look great in it. Their car must feel amazing underneath them, they probably feel the power under their feet, how incredible that must feel. They are lucky they gained, received that beautiful house, I love it!*

To attract and feel comfortable with wealth, and abundance we need to flow into appreciating others' wealth and therefore it brings more to us, it is a full-circle experience. We can start to remove the resistance to money flowing in as we release any limiting beliefs about our own money and others' money. I have seen from experience in working with clients and myself that where the money is not flowing, there is almost always resistance.

When people around me made comments about others' money in disgust or in a negative way, this also pointed out to me *how I still had resistance in myself to related to others' money*. More healing was needed for me to release to come to the philosophy I have now, and to fully embody my healthy money mindset. Otherwise, they would not have felt comfortable making these comments around me, there must have been something to hook into. *As I healed myself from having any resentment towards other peoples' inflow of money, and however they had it, I allowed others around me to be more comfortable with money too.* It was almost miraculous how others' stopped making these types of negative comments regarding others' wealth around me, as there was no place for those comments to stick anymore.

I believe we chose our families of origin for the lessons we need to learn in this life, however, we do not have control over which families we are born into at the beginning. However, we do have control over which stories or perspectives we choose to embody, and patterns and dynamics we are bringing into our lives. It is strenuous to unravel generational patterns, sometimes going through this process feels similar to trying to stop a bad habit or peeling an onion with every layer making us cry. Especially when the patterns we are unraveling is all we have ever known as the truth, this can feel as our whole world is crumbling. Please understand if it does feel your whole world is crumbling as you find your philosophies, unravel patterns, and disrupt generational dynamics, most likely next there will be a chance to rebuild and REDEFINE. We must seek out outside forces in mentors and books to bring awareness to our patterns related to how we are living our lives, and the stories we are choosing to believe.

These ladies here, the co-authors in REDEFINE are a great place to start, they and I offer a wealth of knowledge in REDEFINING and scaling your life, love life, business, and more. *We often have the power to alter our perspectives and stories in any situation.* When we REDEFINE our stories, patterns, and perspectives we give ourselves the power to regain our strength to decide and to be in our heart enacting plus *responding* from a new place. This place feels grounded, centered, strong, trusting, intuitive, radiating, affluent, self-loving...*it is up to you to REDEFINE how this place feels for you. We can decide how we want to feel.*

If we continue to unconsciously be in similar patterns to what we saw growing up we most likely will be in *reactionary mode.* Please remember *there is a space between the stimulus and our reaction, in this space, we can grow into deciding how we will respond.* Going from reacting mode to now being in responding mode in life, is freedom. Also, in this process, we are confirming all of our biases until we become aware. To give an example of this, until I was fully aware of my past resentment I had towards others' having money or of them growing up with a lot of money while I did not grow up this way, hence I was unconsciously attracting friends to me with these similar stories or patterns. The stories and people we attract can start to be cemented or reaffirm our beliefs because we seek out, unconsciously, news sources, stories, and people who will validate them.

Until we are aware and start the process of healing these wounds and traumas, then we can transform them into new beliefs, for them to become new patterns. Also, these are becoming new patterns for generations after we create new beliefs for ourselves! This doesn't mean all of our outside influences have to change, it means our inside world *must* change over time, with immense reflection. We start to influence and impact our outer world because our inner world is healthy. I have been referred to as a *pattern disruptor* before and was proud of someone telling me this in a complimentary way. This trait of mine promotes guidance and transformation for my clients as they REDEFINE what they desire for their lives and then we scale their online businesses with these exact desires coming into fruition. We have the power to transform our outer world. Once we have become aware of our patterns, take responsibility for them, and learn and unlearn them all of this *amplifies* to us seeing what we truly desire come to fruition in our lives.

Our words are powerful.

Therefore, if we are constantly commenting on how we dislike someones' money, negatively referring to how they got it, showing disdain for their material wealth or wealth in general, we are *not* going to bring in those exact things we might desperately be craving. This process calls me to go inwards, the only way to be able to alter my outer world is to alter my inner world. Also, for myself to take full responsibility for my experiences, what the lesson was in them, how they affected me, and then to create new stories and beliefs.

Transforming the pain into healing and wisdom. This does not mean I am perfect in my money mindset by any means, I am always growing too! I do sometimes catch myself if I need to rephrase my words once I realize how they might affect the outcomes directly. *Please remember that continuous suffering and worry bring only more suffering.* What brings *more* success is us starting the journey of removing patterns and creating new beliefs and stories around suffering and living in abundance, and of living in our REDEFINED success for ourselves and our lives.

As I healed myself from having any resentment towards other peoples' inflow of money, and however they had it, I allowed others around me to be more comfortable with money too.

— ALLISON RAMSEY

Allison Ramsey is the founder of Empire Life, a tech and digital marketing company. At Empire Life, female founders are guided in scaling their online empires. Empire Life guides clients in business, sales, tech, and digital marketing strategies, and also has done for you services in designing a seamless user experience and technical infrastructure for membership sites, sales funnels plus scales momentum with Facebook and Google Ads, SEO, and Google Analytics.

Allison is also a software developer, data scientist, and college professor of Facebook Digital Marketing and Data Analytics.

Allison hosts wildly listened to podcasts, The Empire Life Podcast. On the Empire Life podcast founders from all around the world are interviewed on how they built and scaled their successful online empires. Tune in on Spotify, and iTunes, at Empire Life Podcast.

Another sought-after part of Empire Life is the Empire Life Blog. The articles gain tons of exposure and engagement every day. Each author in this book is featured there too. https://www.empirelifeacademy.com/category/blog/

Allison is an experienced international speaker on topics such as women in tech, entrepreneurship, business, leadership, community, scaling empires, and business relationships and partnerships. She enjoys spending time with her loved ones in her free time.

MEGAN COREY

There I was, wearing my A-line dress, suit jacket, heels, hair washed and curled, shoulders up and back, just exuding confidence. I thought I'd made it. I worked hard. I was extremely disciplined and determined. I worked my way up the corporate ladder. Where I always dreamed I'd be. I never really knew what I was going to be when I grew up, but I knew I was going to be successful.

I grew up in a small town in Pennsylvania. The town where everyone knows one another, waving at the on-coming cars because you probably knew them. Since there wasn't a big city around, my entire family ended up being teachers. My family was cut from the same cloth. Mom and Dad were teachers, raising four children, my two sisters, and a little brother. All my siblings grew up to become teachers and live close to each other. Mom and Dad have lived their entire lives in a 10-mile radius and my little brother and one of my older sisters remains in the same vicinity.

I was determined to move away. To do something else with my life. To be something bigger…whatever that was.

I went to the University of Maryland, in Baltimore County, on a swimming scholarship. Actually, I didn't go far away, but at least I got out of the state *and* was close to two big cities. I graduated with an Economics degree because I still didn't know what exactly I wanted to do with my life, but business seemed to be the best route.

After graduation, I worked as a recruiter and manager of a home healthcare agency. Working long hours, commuting, and basically killing myself slowly through a continuous lack of sleep, happy hours, and an abundance of stress. I knew I couldn't keep up the pace or my dreams of starting a family and having some type of personal life were non-existent.

I went the complete opposite way. I went into the federal government. talk about a 180. The pace was way slower than what I was used to, but that's what I wanted, wasn't it? I thought I was going into a job that would help me achieve that work-life balance that everyone dreams about, yet at what cost does that come?

The work was fine. I made a lot of great friends. Had a lot of great mentors looking out for me, but something was missing. It was not one particular thing or day, but that something was missing kept creeping up in my mind. I felt like I was losing a piece of myself every time I walked into the office. *Is this what I'm going to be doing for the rest of my life? Is this worth it to leave my kids every day? Is this the life I pictured?*

It wasn't, but took me a long time to figure out why. *To figure out, if this wasn't it, then what was I meant to do?* I mean I can't just high tail it out of here. I have a family to support. I'm loyal to my job. I worked hard to get where I was. *Do I just throw it all away? To do what?*

I still didn't know. I felt lost. I envied those that were working in their dream jobs. Where "it's not really a day of work if you love what you do," *I mean who even created this phrase, anyways? Is that even possible?* It has to be. I knew I was destined for something big. *Why am I selling myself short by staying in a job I didn't truly love or have a passion for?* I was good at it, but that doesn't always equal passion or purpose.

Something had to change. I was now coming home to my family extremely stressed out every day. I was unhappy. I was sad. I wasn't me anymore. Little things set me off all the time and then I was yelling at my husband and kids for no reason. Who was I becoming? I used to be carefree, happy, and motivated. I didn't like who I was becoming.

My husband didn't either, he said, "Figure something out because you can't keep this up and you're obviously not happy."

Oh no, he was right. My kids knew it too. Mommy was so caught up that she was taking it out on everyone else. Also, my patience and my confidence were super low. In those moments, my mind was talking me out of everything I thought I could do. I had reached a point of feeling comfortable in a certain area, and thinking about doing anything outside of that box seemed almost impossible. My creativity was getting sucked out of me when I stayed doing the same thing for so long. My vision of the future started to look meek. If I continued to let all of this happen, these events would ruin my life. I was talking myself out of anything that was outside of my comfort zone, and of anything that created waves. Also, of anything that would possibly make me happier.

I had to take control. If there was anything I was, it wasn't someone who lays down and accepts things the way they are. I've always been a fighter and I wasn't going to stop now. Especially not when I was only in my mid-30's for God's sake. Could I really just cruise by in life the way it is for another 20 years until retirement? *Hell no.* Then, I started really looking into myself. I started looking at what I loved to do and looking at what else I could do with my life. Then it hit me, I started to notice my surroundings more, and they did have an impact on my life.

Seeing people angry, stressed out, sick, tired, sad, or unhealthy, wasn't ok for me. I started thinking to myself: *Why was everyone acting like their life was terrible? Why were they so unhappy? Why doesn't anyone laugh or smile anymore?* I started observing the people around me more. I was seeing anger in their eyes. I observed people while driving and for example stepping on the gas when someone put on their blinker so they don't have to let them in. Possibly they are angry because their commute is two hours and they are sitting in traffic. I also noticed angry people in meetings. They would be drinking an extra large soda with a kit kat because they were exhausted and didn't make time to eat lunch. In the workplace I observed co workers yelling at each other because they couldn't work together or come to an agreement. Sometimes, it requires one person to be the better person and for everyone to come out ahead. I analyzed some people who feel they just have to win, and no matter the cost. *Is this where my life was taking me? Is this how I was going to act if I remained in these situations?* I said no to myself, it's not, it can't be, and I wasn't ok with this. Not only did I not want to become one of those people, I also wanted to help them.

I thought to myself: *How could I help them? Where do I even start? It feels there are quite a few people lost in their own worlds, will they even want to listen to anyone else? Has anyone ever listened to them? Like truly listened to what was going on in their lives? Why were they so tired? Why were they so sad and angry?*

I was listening, and without even knowing it, I became their sounding board. I was and always have been a people person. I could talk about anything with anyone, and I just talked and listened. I asked questions, I provided guidance, sometimes it was personal, professional, or just general health related recommendations. I saw the effect of my guidance on co-workers, friends, and family. I saw how sometimes being available for them to reach out to was all that was needed. I saw how things I already did and recommended to others was actually helping them over time. I have a strong passion for health and wellness. I started to ask myself: *What does health and wellness mean to me? How or can I make a job out of this? Is this something that people do and get paid for? How can I take my passion and create a living out of this? What was out there for me? Where do I even start?* I always kept my health and wellness as a top priority, even as a working mom, I was creative in how I went about it. I wanted to help others do the same. As I launched into creating my health and wellness business, my mind swirled with ideas. I started researching, mostly going down the self-improvement route. I read books, listened to podcasts, looked into additional training courses, and certifications. I read about finding my passion and purpose in life and figuring out ways to do it. I figured out how to set myself up to transition from my 9 am to 5 pm full-time job. All while fulfilling my passion and my purpose which is so much more meaningful for me than a paycheck.

I figured it out, I was going to be a health coach. This was because of my love for helping people with their overall health and wellness and for desiring to improve my health and wellness and also my family's. I grew up as an athlete, I coached before, and I knew the impact coaching had on the lives of others. I started to seek out a way to integrate this with my love for health and wellness, which felt like a win-win. I wasn't even sure what I was going to do as a health coach, however I knew I had to take the first step and sign up for the certification. I researched a plethora of institutions and found one that would work with my schedule and was focused on a more holistic approach to nutrition and wellness. Their definition of holistic is: taking into account the entire person and everything in their life instead of just one part. I desired to dig into this more and understand why we do the things we do. I started to ask myself: *Why were we becoming a society that continued to kill ourselves through diet, stress, and our overall lifestyle choices?*

It was a tough year, I was working my full-time job, a mom to two small boys, and now going back to school in an opposite direction of my professional life. This was an opposite direction from what I've been working up towards the last 15 years of my life. I thought: *Am I crazy? Why do I think I can do this? Am I a bad mom for wanting to take a risk and take time away from my family to pursue my passion?*

This circled my brain every day, yet didn't tell everyone what I was doing, only some close friends because I was scared. I didn't even know how to tell them I was going to be a health coach. I already had a great job. I didn't want to tell them, and then hear them say to me I was making a bad decision. Some generations feel more comfortable to stay in the same job for 30 plus years and retire there, as I reflected on this, I wasn't ok with this path.

I hustled, while completing my certification I continued on the self-improvement route. I was continuously reading, listening, and learning. If I was going to do this, I needed to figure out what it would look like, and where and how I would start.

I started first by registering my LLC at the end of 2018. I got the word out about what I was doing by hosting local workshops and integrating my services with local businesses. I started with coaching family and friends as clients, to continue to get experience, and then I started taking on private clients. I launched group coaching programs. I hired someone to help me with increasing my social media presence for people to know what I was doing, and to share and educate people on wellness. I did all of this in the morning before I left for work, at night when I put the kids down, and on the weekends. It was *hard*. If anyone tells you having a side hustle with everything else I listed above is easy, they're lying.

I just kept going, and I didn't take time to stop and think, "what if this doesn't work out?" I got scrappy, putting up a basic website, got a basic logo, and just launched. I told myself, this doesn't have to be perfect, but I just needed to start. If I never started, I'd be in the same place I was before. I'd be wondering what I could be doing, unhappy with where my life was, and dreaming of something bigger.

The good thing was, as competitive as I have always been, I'm also ok with failing. I was growing during my time of researching self-improvement techniques. I was understanding where to put my focus, what to wait on, and I was learning a lot while trying to enjoy the ride at the same time. I didn't look back, and I still don't. Progress may not always be forward moving, but in those days I just kept going. I felt the worst that could happen was I'd fall on my face and have to change directions. A lot of what I was doing was trial and error, and I need to be ok with failing and improving.

I was growing professionally and personally during that year and building my business. I was becoming more open-minded, less judgmental, patient, and mindful. I was working on myself constantly, which in turn was helping me work on my business. My creativity, which I temporarily thought was gone while in my full-time job, was then starting to literally come out of my ears. I had ideas coming at me day and night and I'd make lists and add to them all day long. I'd find myself daydreaming and thinking of a new idea. I was finally feeling full of life, and was starting to feel like myself again.

With building a business and having everything else going on in my life, I only had so much room. My focus that year was on business and family. I didn't have time for much else. My social life was nothing like it used to be. I wasn't there for friends all the time and had to say no to a lot. I just couldn't keep up with all of it. I felt guilty from being away from my family when it involved anything else outside of me building my business. I had to prioritize the things that were going to propel me forward in building my business and balance that with making sure my family was still my top priority.

There were so many times that I thought to myself: *Is it worth it Megan? Are you making the right decision? Why not just continue with life as it is and accept that?*

What's funny is I really never had doubts. I don't know if it was the mindset work I was doing, the developmental work on myself, or the fact that I kept telling myself this is what I want, this will eventually be better for me and my family. I was getting the time and freedom back that I was searching for outside of being in a normal full-time job. The location independence as a health coach gave me the incredible job flexibility to make my own schedule.

Being able to make my own schedule is primarily what kept me going and knowing there was something out there to allow me this freedom. In order to work for myself, make my own decisions based on what was best for my family, the flow of figuring it all out came quickly. Lessons I learned growing up gave me the gumption to overcome any bumps, holes, and dead ends along the way. As my mindset evolved I noticed playing the victim or playing small shifted into letting go of jealousy and envy of others. Or, you can pull up your big girl panties, take ownership, take action, and make shit happen on your own.

I wanted to make shit happen, therefore I worked on how to do this everyday. Instead of listening to music or watching Netflix in my free time, I listened to self-improvement books or podcasts on mindset shifts, business, marketing, and just overall life lessons. I was super disciplined because I felt I had to be. If I wanted to make anything of myself, to completely change the direction of my life, to truly start living the life of my dreams, then I had to make the sacrifices to make that happen.

As I write this, this past year has been one of transition and have found creative ways to find time to build my business. I reached out to experts knowledgeable in areas I was either lacking in or just didn't have the bandwidth to focus on. My valuable time was needed to develop my content, and to focus on the business side of things only I could do.

I reached out to business owners during this time, to ask questions, go over ideas, and seek guidance and mentorship. These were successful business owners, therefore this was me asking for help instead of aiming to go about my business development without direction. I figured out how to prioritize the things that I needed to do in order to build my business. I did these things in the morning before I went to work: I'd wake up super early, work about an hour, work out, get ready for work, get my kids ready for school, and then go to work for an entire day. Then, pick up the kids on the way home, get home and make dinner, hangout with the family, get kids ready for bed, get everything ready for the next day, and then work again on my business development. Those were just the weekdays, and on the weekends I'd try to make sure I focused on my family and then one day on the weekend work on my business. This last year had the most hard and trying times. While I was stuck up in my office working and hearing the kids laughing and running around, I had many guilt-ridden moments. This is what went through my head, *"I should be down there with them, playing. I work all week, and now I'm working on the weekend. I should be there for them"*. I just kept telling myself, this will all be worth it, and it won't be like this forever.

Once I understood the areas I needed to focus on to make a name for myself, then I made sure I was connecting with the right people. I set up some in-person workshops with local networking groups, yoga studios, and corporations to give me the opportunity to interact with interested organizations and networks. I'd talk about wellness, weight loss, stress, exercise, good habits, lifestyle, and everything else important in health and wellness. These events brought in private clients, recommendations, and referrals. I would do these sessions in the evening after work, after the kids went to bed, or on the weekends.

I merged the gap in creating group programs from my corporate and group program experience. Being in a group program with others going through something similar to you can be motivating and beneficial to your progress and growth. Having connections and relationships with others which is what we desire and need in our lives. The support and accountability from your peers and a coach has been proven to push you further towards hitting your goals and being successful.

I saw the need for virtual programs as all of my clients, including me, were extremely busy and had no time to go and meet somewhere for a wellness session. It was more convenient to be able to do a phone call, a video call, or have everything at our fingertips through an online platform or email. This made it easy to coach from anywhere and saved me and my clients time instead of driving somewhere or finding a place to meet.

The best part about this was seeing the progress my clients were making in their lifestyle choices, the happiness they were exuding, the way they were feeling in their minds and their bodies. I was helping and guiding them in this! I was working with each of them to come up with realistic habits and lifestyle changes they could make in their lives to start seeing results and start feeling the effects in their life. In hearing their success stories about the changes they were making each day in particular areas of their life, and in being more aware of the choices and decisions they were making with the continued new knowledge gained from our sessions.

After each client session, I was on a high because I had the opportunity to talk about things I was truly passionate about and help others in the process. I never gave myself credit before for what I knew about health and wellness and how successful I had been focusing on this in my life. The fact that I could now coach and help others on their health and lifestyle journeys and be doing this as a job was still unbelievable to me. Yet at the same time, I saw such a need for this type of help because people wanted my help, were overstressed, exhausted, and overwhelmed to know where to start or what to do. These people, my ideal clients, found it extremely difficult to even think they could find ways to be healthy in their crazy and busy schedules. Whether it be wellness, business, or something else in your life, sometimes we can't see outside of the box we're in. We sometimes think we're stuck in what we're doing and there's no way out because we often can't see the way out. That's why we need someone to help, guide, and support us in taking action. With this support we can make changes that create lasting life long habits. Then these habits are just a part of our life.

I find having a health and wellness coach is similar to having a personal trainer or an athletic coach. There's a reason you reach out to these people. There's a reason you get better. There's a reason you show up. You have someone guiding, supporting, and holding you accountable. I was meant to step into the role of pushing others to do better and do big things.

Throughout my year of working my full-time job and building my business, I still had grey areas of what my future would look like.

How could I make enough money to support me and my family with my business? How could I leave a great, stable paycheck for unknown territory? How was I going to make this work?

While still figuring it out, I needed to get creative to bring money in for our needs and my business expenses. Then, I started another business. I know what you're thinking: How does that give you more time or money? I realized I had a lot of knowledge from my corporate job, and it would be a shame for it to go to waste. I also realized the part I liked about my corporate job was networking, building relationships, and helping others. Therefore, why not use this experience and start something where I could do consulting.

Doing consulting allowed me to have less concern over leaving my full-time job because I would have more money coming in while building my wellness business. Consulting allowed me to plan the hours I worked and not be tied to an office setting five days a week, and eight hours a day. Being able to plan my schedule as a consultant gave me the time and location independence I was looking for.

I was lucky enough to do consulting with some organizations on their business development as soon as I left my other job. Others also became interested in my talents and I began to see how this was profitable for me. These opportunities made me feel less scared to finally leave my full-time job. I notified my manager about the possibility of me leaving. My coworkers and management were extremely supportive of me pursuing my passions and my dreams. However, the lingering question from my team kept coming up, 'how long are you here for?' Ironically, I kept pushing the date back in my head of when I will be ready to leave. I was getting scared, as this shit was getting real for me.

After finally looking at dates, looking at the next year, and coming to a realization within myself of how I had to cut the umbilical cord at some point. The truth was, if I wanted to grow, I had to set a date. I started telling people when I would for sure be leaving my full-time job. I told my job the exact date, and my friends, it was scary to say it out loud.

I thought to myself: *Why do I care so much about what others think?* Then I discovered it's in my nature to care, and possibly it is in your nature to care too. Becoming an entrepreneur is outside of the norm for most people, therefore I thought people wouldn't understand my choices. I often thought they would worry about me and the family and judge me because of my new career choice. *But guess what?* As I told a lot of people about my dreams, passions, and new career choice, they were excited for me. They were actually intrigued by what was to come, and thrilled I was making the jump and pursuing my dreams.

This is why I'm encouraging you to follow your dreams, passions, and do things *just for you sometimes*. We need to make decisions that are best for us. In my journey, I did my research, and didn't decide on a whim, a lot of my success came through planning and working hard. I set myself up for success before I decided to leave my full-time job. Also, my husband was supportive, which honestly was the most important for me. He was the one pushing me to do better, to do what I loved, and to think bigger. Without his support, encouragement, and consistent presence and belief in my business, I don't know where I'd be.

There were many people I came across in my journey asking me, "Well what does your husband think of all this? You leaving a good-paying job to start a business?"

To which I often replied, "He's actually the one pushing me and is super supportive."

He and I made my business goals together. First, we figured out our finances to see what it would look like if we only had one paycheck coming in, and then we cut back on travel, expenses, and anything that was nonessential. We aimed to be prepared for anything life will throw at us. In retrospect, I feel planning everything out ahead of time makes things a lot less scary, and makes everything seem doable. Having a plan prevents me from losing my shit daily because of thinking about the future.

Don't get me wrong, I was a stress ball to the max during this time of my life. My stress was showing through my face breaking out, weight going up and down, and brain racing constantly. But, in the back of my mind, I knew it wouldn't be like this forever, and I told myself this is *just something I was going through now.* I was setting myself up for success so I wouldn't continuously be in the grind and knew it would all pay off someday.

My life was extraordinarily busy while leading up to the date of leaving my job, I was ramping up in my business, and getting out there more. Yet at the same time, with being in my integrity, I wanted to make sure the job I was leaving was situated and work could go on without me in the office. I didn't want to leave them on bad terms, I had an amazing team, and I wanted to make sure they were set up for success with or without me remaining on the team. The last two weeks prior to leaving my full-time job ended up feeling like a complete mind F. This is because I felt torn between two completely different jobs and this *just made my brain hurt daily.* I felt as if I had one foot in one area and one foot in another area, and this made me feel pulled in multiple directions. However it did make my life a little easier to hear everyone at work was excited for me, some were envious that I was making the jump, and yet most felt happy for me. They told me they were happy for me because I was taking the leap to pursue my passions and purpose in life, and that they'd been afraid to leap themselves or didn't think they could ever do it. This whole process of exiting my previous company was bittersweet for me. I had no hard feelings, only positivity and good vibes.

For most of my life, I had been hustling, with my business as my side hustle. I'd read that it's tricky to really push your business forward and stop treating it like a side hustle once you can actually put more time towards it and did not want to fall into that trap. I wanted to continue the progress I was making and not let my momentum stop, therefore I kept pushing. I kept putting myself out there, reaching out to more people for partnerships, and being open to new things that might come along. I felt excitement, stress, and fear all at the same time, in a beautiful mixture.

With my momentum coming in at full force this in turn brought more opportunities. It seemed that things were falling into place as they should after I left my full-time job because I started taking on more clients, partnering with more businesses, and becoming more creative in building my business. Sometimes I will change directions a little bit and continue to pivot when needed in my business. What my business looks like now, or what it will look like in one year, will most likely be somewhat different because I continue to grow, evolve, and thank for being on this journey with me. I give myself patience because everyone when first starting is green in the business area, and have learned a lot over this past year. I've grown, failed, and made mistakes, yet am continuously learning from those mistakes.

My growth is often the biggest reason in propelling my business forward. Often I thought to myself: *What if I was still a perfectionist? What if I didn't know how to accept defeat? Would I even want to keep going each time something went south? How would I even know what to do in those situations?* If I was still feeling these ways, who knows if I will have continued to grow. The truth is, I didn't know how everything would work out, but I did know I would figure it out. Sadly, I understood the world is not all rainbows and unicorns daily, and often we don't know everything all the time. I mean this sounds awesome if life were rainbows and unicorns yet it is totally unrealistic to believe it is! The real story I feel is, failing is learning, learning is growth, and growth gives the motivation to keep going, even in tough times.

For me, this motivation brings creativity and I was becoming more creative each day with every thought. Instead of staying in my head and analyzing by asking myself *what if this didn't work out,* I took action on where I needed to adjust, fire, redirect, and make changes. Part of my tools in my success are meditation and yoga, they help me in many ways. I have always felt we are all in a rat race, and this leads us to never stop to actually think or feel about what's going on around us. Our creativity can often be blocked by the daily nonsense of our crazy lives, until we actually stop for a few minutes, take time to breathe, and take time to be more mindful of our actions and thought patterns. A lot of us are in a continuous brain spin of fighting fires of the days' madness that we often cannot see five feet ahead of ourselves. We cannot see how to make a change to create the future we want and deserve, or why we are unhappy or stuck.

Once I got out of my own way I could see my future more clearly. I could envision what the next five years of my life and beyond would look like as an entrepreneur. I was now my own boss, and making the decisions. I was who I've always wanted to become but never knew how to become my own boss. *Was it scary?* It was a little scary, but I don't stop and hide when things get tough or scary. I look for ways around the scared feelings and look for a better way. Asking myself: *Am I doing the best I can in the situation?* If you know you're doing the best you can and you're not making excuses and only finding solutions, you will be *just fine.* This concept is how I manage my life now.

I'm always looking for ways to get myself out there, to expand, and grow. But now I'm getting smarter about it because I'm looking at my effort to the outcome and analyzing this. I ask myself frequently: *Am I truly being the most efficient I can be? Am I making the best decisions for my business that will allow it to continue to grow or is it going to stall my progress? Am I having fun and enjoying the ride or am I waking up dreading another day?* Asking ourselves these questions is super important! Personally, I didn't leave my full-time job to do something I didn't enjoy therefore these questions are always in the back of my head. In desiring to continue pursuing my passions and dreams I always want to make sure to be creating the best balance that I can with business, family, and friends. With where I am in my business as I write this I am experiencing immense fulfillment in bringing in what I want, need, and desire while helping others change their lives.

It's super easy to get caught up in the imposter syndrome and jealousy as we begin being our own boss. We see all of these extremely successful people out there with millions of followers, major deals with big companies, and this starts to make us feel small sometimes. Have you ever found yourself asking questions such as: *What do I know compared to him or her? Could I ever be that successful? What they're doing takes more hours in the day than I have, could I ever do that?* You know what, this type of thinking puts us in victim mode and will often stop us in our tracks. Luckily, I experienced all of this and continued to press on. As I write this, recently, I was being interviewed on a podcast and they asked me: *What goes through your mind when you see others doing the same things you do out there?* My answer was: I'm different, we're all different, and all have something unique to bring to the table. Here is how I am different, it is in the way I coach, my experiences, my training, and my personality, well they're unlike anyone else's! The good news is, neither are you, you are you, and only one of you exists in this world. There's a reason people want to work with me, heck, there is also a reason people want to be friends with me it is because they appreciate and enjoy me. Also, I am a realist and don't take any shit. I really try not to complain, am upbeat about life, and truly enjoy pushing others to be their best just as I do for myself.

This is why I love wellness, good habits, and lifestyle coaching and facilitating this for my clients. With doing all of this for my clients they see progress in their health, their lives, and in their organizations. In guiding my clients to be their best selves, I have discovered ways as a busy working mom to always put my health and wellness as a priority in my life and I want to help others do the same. I have programs that work for the busiest of busy executives and professionals. We focus on lifestyle choice, habits, and making small changes, this leads to a big payoff. I get in life there often feels like no extra time to have to drive somewhere to be coached this is why all of my programs and appointments are virtual. Furthermore often there is no time to make meals, this is why I focus on being healthy while eating out, there's no elimination, no fad diets, or no unrealistic changes I ask of my clients. This is why my programs work, for me and those I coach.

My clients see how life becomes better when they start to become more aware, this awareness is about their environment, stressors, patterns, and decisions. I feel becoming aware of all of these is the first step in completely changing our lives. In walking my own talk, I am also always bringing more awareness to my life. Bringing more awareness in these areas really works for me and has helped me grow and learn, and I feel this can work for anyone looking to make changes in their life. These changes can be personal or professional and awareness is the first step to make that change. From this point, I usually start to see things fall into place the way I feel they should because the decisions I make are the right ones for the path I want to see in front of me. In having these thought processes for myself, this is how I continue to grow personally and in my businesses.

My concepts are not rocket science or magic, and I feel it's all already inside of you. You are going to make the choices needed to improve your life because you know innately what's best for you. Hopefully by this point in my story, you're now more aware of why and how you're doing what you're doing, then I am sure doors will start flying open for you and your creative brain is thriving with ideas. As you pursue your passions and dreams your body and soul will be fulfilled and you will be living life by your rules.

It took me until my late 30's to finally figure all of this out, but I am glad I didn't wait any longer than this. I was not ok with just being ok, and am proud of myself for taking the bull by the horns. I am proud of myself for starting my own business and this process was not pretty by any means, and still is not pretty at least half of the time! If I had waited for something pretty or perfect, I may have never done anything at all ever, and that is why I just started. I knew I had to do this for me and my family, and my advice to anyone who is on the fence about their life decisions, where their future is headed, or just finding themselves unhappy or stuck, is to *just* start. Probably the worst that can happen is you fail, fall on your face, or make a bad decision, but you'll never know until you start and until you take the first step. Please be ok with developing yourself along the way and learning as you go, transition slowly, take your time, ask questions, and reach out for help.

I wouldn't be where I am today if years ago I just kept continuing to come home and complain, thinking there's no way I can leave my job and start my own business, feel sorry for myself, and blame everyone else. If I kept listening to that crappy voice in my head, I'd still be in the same job, like a robot, unhappy, and unfulfilled thinking this is what my life is, and being unable to see any other possibilities.

I am happy for the success I've had and I look forward to the future of my life and business. I'm grateful for the support of Empire Life, and Empire Life founder Allison Ramsey in publishing this book, REDEFINE, and the advice I'm continuously given from family, friends, and mentors. I couldn't have done any of this on my own. Yet here is the thing, I wasn't afraid to ask for help when I needed to and wasn't afraid to ask questions to those that are way smarter than I am and have seen success in their businesses because they figured it out. Please don't be afraid to ask, afraid to take chances, or afraid to be happy and fulfill your dreams.

This is your life and don't let anyone else live it. I continue to live by these words and replay them in my head, and live by them *every day*. I dislike having regrets, and that's why I'm always going for my dreams! I want to know, and I want you to know, we've done our best and we are incredibly happy and fulfilled because of it.

If I had waited for something pretty or perfect, I may have never done anything at all ever, and that is why I just started.

— MEGAN COREY

Megan Corey is an executive wellness coach, healthy living expert, published author, and speaker. Megan works with high performers to change habits, shift mindsets, and transform lives.

She knows what it takes to develop and sustain healthy lifestyle habits as a businesswoman, entrepreneur, and working mom. She desires to educate and empower other high achievers to do the same.

Megan believes to truly be successful in all areas of your life and to continue to excel in your career and business, you have to take care of your mind and body. Take care of yourself first and everything else falls into place!

IIYSE CRAFT

THE ABC'S OF BEING A CONSCIOUSLY CONFIDENT ENTREPRENEUR

My name is Ilyse Craft, and I pride myself on making things happen. I have a super high vibe and a distinct knowledge that can be quite infectious. If you dig me, this can be quite intoxicating. If not, it can be annoying.

I dream big, and I am a realist.

Throughout the past few years, I have radically changed my life. I know there have been people that do this in three months, three weeks, or three days. It took me a little longer. I would not change a thing. I wouldn't change anything, partially because I cannot. I have radical gratitude for the life I do have, instead of longing for a life that is not mine.

Let's dig in. Thank you so much for being a part of this journey with all of us. I am so happy you're here. I pray that you gain something from this re-telling. I find storytelling to be one of the most effective forms of coaching and learning. Inside a story, we see glimmers of our current or past selves or ways in which we hope to be one day. I have found ease and grace in sharing pieces and parts of my life with other people. This allows them to be more of themselves, while I too, gain further access to myself. It is the gift that gives permission.

I have learned in this digital worldwide stage, that in some cultures, the phrase *story-telling* means, *making up a story, or telling a lie.* I have learned to speak more broadly on the world stage every time I hit the *LIVE* button on my phone. My videos are reaching millions of people consistently over the past year.

For any of you that have ever thought, *I could never do that* when it comes to making a video or going *LIVE* on a social media platform, I said the same thing. It wasn't just a thought. I said it out loud. I actually judged the people doing it. *Who are they with their 2 cents? What makes them the expert?* Any and every thought that is being thought is not new to this world! Been there, done that, by someone going LIVE and putting themselves out there.

Here is the great news in all of this: in the journey of redesigning and reinventing your life, you meet yourself every step of the way. As an online entrepreneur, I thought I was starting a business. I thought that's what was going to happen here. Little did I know, I was going to learn more about myself in the process, than doing anything else ever in my professional career.

Buckle-up Buttercup.

You are in for the time of your life. I wouldn't want you to miss this for your life. It is the greatest show on earth. You have the starring role. You are the main attraction. It is all about you, all day every day. You think it's about the clients, the product, the offer, the audience, Facebook, the algorithm, this, that, and the other thing. It is all about you. This is the greatest news of all, even when it may not feel that way.

I have had many business ventures in my life, thus far. I love business and my mind never stops. I've had to actively work at the process of *minding my mind* which has been part of my edge in growing myself up. Sometimes, distractions or emotions win. This is why I work with a coach to help me with my mindset, growth, and purpose.

What catapulted my expansion this time was a health scare in the late summer of 2018. I truly believe that a major life event is not necessary, but in case I am wrong, we have all been delivered one with the world events we have all been living through. The pandemic has served as that time in many people's lives to take a deeper look and ask meaningful questions about the choices they have made and the direction they are headed.

Back in 2018, when I had a flurry of unrelated and scary symptoms, all resembling a health scare. There was also a spot on my brain. Let's just say, these are not things you want any part of. After six painfully long weeks, in which I was doing a lot of preparing for my looming departure, I was cleared for living.

Did you hear that? Cleared for living.

I really needed to look at things and pronto.

I started living fully, and never looked back.

Here are the ABC's of Being a Consciously Confident Entrepreneur, while living an awesome life and creating a soon to be multiple six-figure online business. While living an awesome life, in the process I created a soon to be multiple six-figure online business. Currently, I help people fall wildly in love with themselves to become a magnet for everything they deeply desire. I help them *Craft* their *A* plan because there is not any other plan worth going for. In my world, it is all about the vibes, a whole lot of magic, and staying until the credits roll...you do not want to miss a thing.

A - allow and give yourself a chance at the greatest ride of your life. Here's the thing though, you need to get on the ride. If you buy a ticket to Disneyland but you never got on any of the rides, did you experience it? Go all in! What is the point if you show up but don't play all out? Allow yourself the full experience. Go for it. I have clients who work with me and their fear of getting it wrong or of it not working, actually creates the business environment of it not working out. The truth is, we have many things that do not work out....and do work out. You can handle it. When you have someone with you for the ride of your life, it is much easier to navigate the monkeys in your head.

B - becoming - Everyone wants the *Book of How.* Even if I handed over the book of how I hit my first $100K or my first $10K or or or, it really would not matter. It will always and forever be who I became along the way that created success. Grow yourself up, and do the personal development work. Keep discovering who you came here to be. Yes, of course, it takes a strategy. Having a solid, confident constitution to implement the strategy is key. Notice the *ing*. Until I take my last breath, I will keep learning and growing. I pray you will too.

C- confident (of course) - I saw it written that we are not born with confidence, but that it is a skill set that can be learned and developed. I have witnessed my growth and expansion exponentially over the past few years as I have navigated technology, relationships, losses, gains, and expansion with a level of confidence I did not have before. There is outward confidence we show the world and inner strength that is undeniable. My body of work reaches, teaches, and reinforces inner strength. When you surround yourself with like-minded people, this builds you up, and highlights who you truly are. The theory that we are the sum of the five people we spend the most time with has proven to be true. I stand by this fully.

D - devotion - The relationship I have to this word has completely transformed the depth of my commitment and my golden word has become much shinier. Once given, it is kept. When you shift from being devoted to pain, suffering, and the past into joy, love, happiness, celebration, and high vibration, your life will change. Add in becoming increasingly aware of the words you choose and the people you hang out with; you've got a whole new lease on life and business.

E - energy - Low, high, good, and bad. You can feel it when you walk into the room. Energy is something that is a huge part of my success and the field I play in. When you take charge of your energy and realize you are responsible for how you respond to what happens even when bad things occur, your life and results will blow you away.

F - FOMO - This might make you laugh, but having a serious *Fear of Missing Out* can set you back. Trying to jump ahead, taking ridiculous *three steps to overnight success* workshops and never-ending masterclasses can lead you down a rabbit hole. This never-ending cycle possibly only takes you right back where you started from. This fear of missing out causes the very thing you are most afraid of. By having this fear that *everyone* is getting ahead and killing it, somehow they all figured it out and you are missing out, you start doing things to *catch up*. Slow down. Time is an illusion. You are doing great.

G - gladness - Living in anticipation for something incredible to happen is the best feeling. When my daughter moved in during the pandemic, I would update her on a new client signing a contract.

Her response was, "Of course they did!"

We are always in gratitude, and living from celebration to celebration with laughter. Expect and seek miracles and become a magnet to all that you desire.

H - happy - Seems pretty simple and straightforward I know. Yet, this is, shockingly, one of the most important ingredients to any kind of success. Money may not make you happy. It is going to make life a heck of a lot easier. *Happy?* That is something entirely different. What I have come to learn is that happiness resides inside. I had to go inside and cultivate it. Plant seeds. Discover who I am, why I am here, connect with something way beyond me, and allow that source to guide me. I also decided to get honest about what I truly desired; made a business from my desires. I helped other women tap into their desires and use master manifesting powers, gratitude, and celebration to enjoy my life to the fullest.

I - impact - What is this all for anyway? I had to get honest about this. One of the signature questions of my brand is *what do you stand for*, and I help people all over the world answer this question. Whether you want to impact your family, community, or the world, a happy and fulfilled human has a tremendous impact on every person they interact with. Deciding what it is you truly want to do with your life and business right now is a powerful inquiry, and you get to decide it. I am drawn to Mary Oliver's poem, *The Summer Day,* a simple yet powerful quote, "What is it you plan to do with your one wild and precious life?"

L - love/lust - What's love got to do with it? Besides it being a great song title, everything. Literally everything. My take on this is slanted. Sure you want to love your business and I have seen very stressed out, burnt out, and anxiety-driven entrepreneurs making a ton of money. One has to ask, do you love that? Really? When you love yourself and have a lust for life and who you are living it with, you will create a healthy harmony to grow your business. Load up with love and lust for yourself, and let the world respond in kind.

I chose the first 12 letters of the alphabet, representing this past year. It has been a year of tremendous learning. The year began on a spiritual pilgrimage in India for several weeks, to return, at best guess, with a case of undiagnosed COVID-19. It was so early on there were no tests. My bad case of the flu took six weeks to heal from. I immediately got scrappy and leaned in. It's how I am built. It's in my DNA: Destiny. Nature. Authentic.

It does not make it right or make me better in some way. It is how I cope. I put my head up, took a deep breath, and got on with it. By late March, I was ready to honor the truth of being in the wrong coaching agreement. After making a financial settlement, I burned it all down and vowed to hire a coach to support me in the way I desired and deserved. That is exactly what I did.

I have been creating and recreating myself as an online entrepreneur. I am always checking in to make sure that what I am doing is of the highest service to myself, my clients, and the impact I desire to have on the world. Within a short amount of time, I have elevated my digital footprint to be seen all over the globe. I am helping people become abundantly clear why they are here, and what they truly want to do. As I write this I am about to launch my own App, Manifesting Miracles, my podcast, LinkedIn show, and YouTube channel. I also hope as I am writing this I will have already accomplished doing a TedX Talk. What I stand for is mission accomplished.

I stand for visibility for millions, and I begin with one. I have always been that person who sees the one person who is not included, sometimes that one person who is off to the side. I feared being that person, after a childhood bike accident.

Similar to Beyonce, I created an alter ego and became an overly friendly, outgoing, funny, sweet kid. Truth be told, I was hurting and felt pretty bad inside about the way I looked after the accident. The fear of being left out and wanting to belong was the first strategy I ever created. I have radical gratitude for all the things that have happened. I cannot go back and change them. Neither can you. An accident from childhood has become the work I do today. I often meet clients who use a lot of emotional energy trying to hide pieces of their past. There are parts of their lives they feel are too shameful, whether it is divorce, bankruptcy, getting fired, or the way they handled certain times in their life.

These are the parts of ourselves that are our greatest gifts. The parts that others bond with. The parts of themselves they find woven into their stories. The way you lead yourself forward and the life you create is everything and all there is.

What I am most proud of is my ability to teach you how to stay when others cannot or will not. I pride myself in guiding others in learning how to stay in the conversation, in the thought, in momentum, in trust, in *it,* long enough to work through it, to redefine their lives.

All it takes is one powerful decision.

You choosing you.

Slow down. Time is an illusion. You are doing great.

— IIYSE CRAFT

I'm Ilyse Craft, a beautiful mix of hippie, happy, and wildly driven to live life purely by my heart's desire. A very new and crazy fun concept after spending 33 years in corporate America.

I was well paid to drive profitable sales, all the while trying to prove my worth. Little did I know then, that was never going to be the place I would find it.

After a health scare and heartache, I decided since I was going to live, to actually do just that.

MINDY GREEN

A LOVE LEGACY

This is a story of love, connection, and the meaning of life. I knew immediately after reading the quote below that it described how I felt about my life. It resonated deeply. Maya Angelou's quote, "My mission in life is not merely to survive, but to thrive; and to do so with some passion, some compassion, some humor, and some style," it has been my lifelong desire to live a life full of purpose, joy, and to build a life surrounded by the people I love while doing meaningful work. The belief I am made for more than simply surviving each day has helped me to stay focused even when there have been unexpected twists in the road.

Looking back on memories and lessons from childhood, it is interesting what bubbles up. The common thread entwined through it all is love and a connection between me and the past and who I am in the present day. I have always loved listening to the family stories of those who died long before I was born. I have often envisioned them surrounding me with love, guidance, comfort, and providing me with a foundation to build my own story, part of the legacy of love for future generations.

Growing up in a small, rural community in Delaware with a large extended family, my family felt like it was meant to be. In my community one was known by who your family was. The family was important and there was a sense of honor, responsibility, duty, and care and support for one another. The motto, albeit unspoken, was, "family first." My family was the backdrop for every major gathering, celebration, and holiday tradition. Besides my parents and sister, my significant relationships were with my grandparents, aunts, uncles, and cousins. These interactions were the framework of my world.

At an early age, I was aware of my mother's struggles with depression and anxiety. Having dealt with postpartum depression after my sister and I were born, it was a lifelong issue for her and impacted our family in both large and small ways. She gave up her job as a high school history teacher to stay home. My father chose to leave his job as a middle school principal and became a farmer to have more flexibility to be available to my mom. With the change in jobs, it created some financial hardships.

"Damn sun worshippers", was one of my dad's often repeated phrases in the summertime.

Frustration over the lack of rain for his crops, his comments were directed at the tourists who would travel to the beaches near our home for their vacations. According to him, each year seemed to be worse than the last with the challenges of the weather, crop prices, and the expense of replacing aging equipment. Seeing his stress, I associated owning a business with risk and financial insecurity.

Along with the values of family duty and hard work, education was another priority. How could it not be with two parents who were educators! Doing well academically was an expectation. Although my parents never said it out loud, yet college was always the next step for us kids. While the dream for my future wasn't well-formed, I knew I wanted to attend college, have a successful career, and raise a family of my own.

One of the defining moments in high school happened in my junior year as those of us interested in college gathered in the library to take the PSAT. While we were filling out the registration forms, I came to the part asking what college major I wanted to choose. I remember so clearly the confusion I felt because I had no idea what I wanted to do.

Tentatively I raised my hand and asked, "What if I don't know what I want to do?"

Very quickly the counselor responded, "Well if you don't know what you want to do why are you going to college?"

Embarrassed and feeling a bit stupid, I wondered if I was the only one who didn't know what I wanted to do for the rest of my life. At

17, the rest of my life seemed like an eternity. Frantically looking over the options listed, I ended up choosing psychology, partly to have something filled in, and partly because of my mom's mental health issues. That one brief decision of choosing this major led to a great college experience. The college I went to ended up being close to home and I thrived in that environment. The psychology department had just expanded to offer a bachelor's degree and the professors were excited to welcome our class as the first ones to go through the four-year program. My advisor, a thin, nervous-looking man, took a special interest in us and his long, spirited conversations with us about psychology theories and human behavior brought to life the information we were learning about in our textbooks. His classes were my favorite because he knew the material inside and out and his lectures were interesting and humorous. I enjoyed choosing classes on topics I was interested in and having the freedom to make my own decisions.

Graduate school was my next step, and it took me further away from home to Baltimore, Maryland. In my second year, I was in an inner-city social work internship and at the school, the students were dealing with eye-opening issues: poverty, death, gang fights, drugs, addiction, and PTSD. It felt like I had jumped from the frying pan into the fire, but I loved the school environment and the students. It led to my first job at the school and I was stretched way out of my comfort zone. I was getting used to living in the city, exploring with my friends, and developing a network. I was challenging myself to think in a completely different way than I had before and develop my own identity as a young woman with a career.

An excited phone call from one of my best friends from college announcing her engagement led to a chance meeting with her cousin. He and I began to talk regularly, and these conversations led to a marriage proposal a year later. By the spring, I was planning my move to Virginia and interviewing for new jobs.

Within a month of moving, I was offered a job. It was different from what I had been accustomed to in Baltimore. These students and their families were upper-middle class, wealthy, and living high stress and high profile lives. The kids had been in and out of mental health treatment programs, knew all of the therapeutic lingo, and were bored and jaded by their experiences. It required a new level of knowledge and expertise on my part. Even though my time in Baltimore City had been tough, the new environment was tougher. I had to develop new skills and approaches to meet the students' and parents' needs. My hour-long drives home were filled with regular pep talks and a few tears.

One of my dreams was to have a larger family of my own, so shortly after my husband and I were married, I became pregnant with our first daughter. On one of the hottest days of the summer, a six-pound baby with a small head (exactly what I asked for by the way) made her way into the world two and a half weeks early. Gazing at my daughter in those moments afterward, I felt like I had come full circle. I felt such intense love and connection to her and my mother. It just happened to be our first wedding anniversary, and as luck would have it, my parents were visiting with us to celebrate our anniversary and ended up being there for the birth of their first grandchild.

Little did I realize how quickly our family would expand. Seven months later I was pregnant with our second daughter and she joined her sister right before Christmas. Having two children under two and working full-time wasn't easy. As much as I had wanted to have a career, it was taking a toll on me. I felt guilty for not being at home with my daughters as my mother had been for me. Yet concern about money prevented me from leaving my job.

I am not sure if we consciously decided to try for a third child, but our son was born two years after his sister. At that point, we had three children aged three and younger. The decision to stay home was a no-brainer at this point. The cost of daycare for three children would have been incredibly high and my salary would only just be enough to cover the costs of childcare.

I vividly remember the lofty plans I had for being a stay-at-home mom: the house would always be clean, all my projects like scrapbooking, learning to sew, would get done, and then I decided I was going to research homeschooling. Not surprisingly, it wasn't as easy of a transition as I had hoped for. Most of my projects didn't get done, I was lonely for adult conversation, we had one car which my husband took to work each day, money was tight, and I mourned my identity as a career woman. What I held onto those days when I was feeling most overwhelmed though was a vision for what I wanted for my family.

When my grandmother died a year later, she gifted us with an older, and well-loved car. It was the best present she could have given us. I had my own car again and the kids and I could start plugging into activities. We made friends through a church we joined. Even though I had three children in car seats in the back of a Honda Accord, I felt like the sky was the limit!

About a year later, we traded in our Honda Accord for a minivan and we became minivan owners, something we vowed never to be. Loading up the kids and driving through different neighborhoods looking at single-family homes was my entertainment and a way to get out of the tight space of our townhouse. One day as we were driving, I saw a for sale sign on a house reading, *for sale by the owner*, and decided to call the phone number. I set an appointment for us to look at the house and two months later we moved in. That house has been our home now for twenty years and one of the most powerful examples in my life of manifesting what I wanted!

When my oldest daughter was ready to begin kindergarten, I decided to homeschool her for a year. It would be an experiment to see how it would go and with the understanding that if I didn't screw it up too badly, we may do it longer. Being a researcher by nature, I had read every book I could find at the library and talked to all the homeschool parents I knew. I had high hopes and big plans. When we got about a month into it, we were both frazzled. I felt like I had a lot to prove to my parents who had questioned me about why I wanted to keep her home and my daughter didn't seem to be enjoying my teaching as much as I thought she should. In tears one day, I called a homeschool veteran mom friend I knew. As I poured my heart out to her, I said I was failing at teaching kindergarten.

She kindly listened and then I will never forget what she said, "Mindy, it's kindergarten."

It was then that it struck me, I was missing the whole point of having my daughter at home, and the heart connection we were forming. Somehow my daughter and I both survived that first year of homeschooling. Pregnant with my youngest son and averaging about three hours of sleep a night, I'd often think that it was preparation for what was to come. When he was born, he slept extraordinarily little amounts at a time and cried unless he was being held. During homeschool lessons, I propped him up with blankets and carried him in a backpack. My husband and I frequently joked that our hopes of making a guest appearance on Oprah as parenting experts diminished with the arrival of our fourth child.

My life was happy chaos. Although the house was frequently messy and I had a list a mile long of things to do, I had settled into a nice, workable routine with the kids, homeschooling, and outside activities. I had a supportive network of fellow homeschool moms and was focused on staying strongly connected with my kids and husband.

Around that time my mom was diagnosed with rare kidney disease and was looking at a transplant. The recipient list was long, but she felt positive about going forward with it. A few days after Mother's Day, she was scheduled to begin dialysis. During the days leading up to it, my mom was feeling some anxiety so as a pleasant distraction my sister, daughters, and I planned a brief visit to celebrate Mother's Day with her. Shortly before we arrived, she fell, and my dad decided to take her to the emergency room at the local hospital. Weak and dehydrated, she needed dialysis as soon as possible. She died shortly afterward due to collapsed veins.

When the doctor came out to share the news, I was shell shocked. My mom had fought so many battles in her life and this was the one she lost. I had no idea what to say to my daughters who were staying with my aunt and uncle or to my sons who had stayed home in Virginia with my husband. *How could I tell my children that their grandmother was dead?*

My dad who had been devoted to my mom's care grieved deeply after her death. As he struggled to make sense of his feelings, and deeply changed our relationship. Our daily conversations became tense and my own anxiety started to grow. Panic attacks became a regular occurrence, and I was concerned for myself. *Was I developing mental health issues, too?*

Being heavily involved in my homeschool support group as the newsletter editor and mentor to other families at that time, I felt like I was letting everyone down. I was pretending to be happy and have it all together but in actuality getting out of bed each day was a struggle. *I was at war with myself and my thoughts.* Then one day as I woke up, it hit me that it was okay to ask for help. I decided to set aside the objections in my head and reached out to my doctor to start medication and therapy. It was like a fog lifted and I was able to enjoy life again. As I was settling back into some normalcy, my dad began to complain about feeling rundown. After testing, his doctor found blood clots and over the next week, my dad was diagnosed with stage four pancreatic cancer. Just three and a half weeks after receiving his cancer diagnosis, he died surrounded by our family. I felt out of sync with my cousins and friends whose parents were still living. I was 38 and both of my parents were gone. I spent several months working through the *"why me"* thoughts I was having and deep feelings of resentment.

Everything felt heavy: relationships, homeschooling, and especially figuring out how to settle my dad's estate. My stress levels were extremely high, and I knew I needed support to manage the physical symptoms I was experiencing. I didn't want to go back on medication, after researching different options, I sought out an alternative treatment from a functional nutritionist. Her attentive approach to uncovering what was going on provided me with the answers I needed to help my body heal. She diagnosed me with adrenal fatigue and through her guidance, I was able to get back on my feet for the next year. As I approached 40 and a new decade, I felt a desire to work on my own personal development. During everything going on for and with my children, it felt like a part of me was getting lost. *Being "mom" and "homeschool mom" was overshadowing anything else in my life.* I decided to take courses to renew my advanced social work license. While the training piqued my interest, I realized the timing was off for me to pursue a career again. When my oldest daughter began high school, our home became even busier. At that point, the kids were in 3rd, 5th, 7th, and 9th grades. It wasn't unusual for us to have extra kids at the house for sleepovers, youth events at church, or other activities. We had an open-door policy and the kids' friends knew they were always welcome and loved. This is something that continues to this day.

Homeschooling became more demanding, and to keep me organized, I created a schedule that my children referred to as, *"The Mother Board"*. My "schedule central" included a calendar and a whiteboard divided into days of the week and was color-coded by a person. It listed everything scheduled for the day and week including work, classes, activities, appointments, and more. Looking back on it now, I am grateful for that bit of divine inspiration. It was a huge time and sanity saver. As my oldest daughter was ready to start her junior year of high school, she very much wanted to attend public school. Although I was hesitant initially, I decided to let her go. My younger daughter had been diagnosed with a juvenile form of arthritis, and with frequent trips to National Children's Hospital in Washington DC for treatment, I needed greater flexibility in my schooling schedule.

With my younger daughter's unexpected diagnosis, I wanted to do everything I could to help her heal. We made radical changes to our home life. What had started as a desire to look for solutions for healthier living sparked a passion to switch out all our cleaning supplies, personal care products, and revamp our eating habits. The kitchen became our lab for our experiments on how to make all our own products. My oldest daughter's high school graduation was a milestone, thirteen years of homeschooling, and the beginning of what I refer to as "The Graduation Years".

Being two years apart in school meant every other year one of the kids would graduate. It was a steep learning curve figuring out the college application process as a homeschool mom, what records to keep, and how to talk to admissions counselors. Guiding my kids through this process felt daunting at times and humbling. Being the one who planned and taught most of their classes, I felt like I was putting my life's work out into the world to be judged.

Some of my favorite memories in recent years have been those college road trips with the kids and our car ride conversations. We laughed and talked about everything from their concerns, interests, and dreams for the future. To be honest, seeing their excitement for college also made me a little sad. Our grand adventure of homeschooling was coming to an end and the big question of what was next loomed over me. The thought of the empty nest years ahead filled me with uncertainty.

As I continued researching diet and lifestyle changes, ads began popping up in my Facebook feed about life and health coaching programs. Curious, I decided to call one of the schools and find out more about what they offered. I hadn't made an investment in myself of this size since before having children. I debated the timing, the cost, whether it was the right school, and if I had what it took to complete the program. Scraping up my courage, I leaped faith and enrolled two weeks later.

Nine months afterward, I finished my coaching program and received my certifications in life and health coaching. I felt accomplished! I was ready to start my coaching business, but I had no idea how. A moment of overwhelming led me to make a Facebook post on a coaching page and a warm, sincere response by another coach led me to my next best investment, hiring a private business coach. Working with her over the past year has led to personal growth well beyond what I could have ever imagined and a clear vision of living a life with passion and meaning.

With the guidance of my coach, I put together an in-person grief group. It was scheduled to begin the first week of March 2020. Then everything shut down due to the pandemic. In the weeks after, we discussed what to do. The idea emerged to shift my focus to provide support for parents who were suddenly thrust into schooling at home from the school closings or considering homeschooling in the fall. As a volunteer counselor with my state homeschool organization, I had several conversations with overwhelmed parents who were seeking ongoing support to figure out their next steps. I knew there was a huge need, and it was a perfect fit for my background.

Now it is my joy to have a coaching business that focuses on empowering and equipping parents with tools to create healthy connections with their children, communicate with confidence, and have peace of mind as they cope with the ups and downs of life. My desire to help parents learn to love and experience the joy of parenting has led to group speaking engagements, being featured in a local newspaper as a homeschool expert, interviews on podcasts, and the creation of a successful masterclass to support moms. Helping parents thrive and be the architects of their own family legacy is the meaningful work I envisioned many years ago and I am excited about the new opportunities to come in the future.

Homeschooling became more demanding, and to keep me organized, I created a schedule that my children referred to as, *"The Mother Board"*.

— MINDY GREEN

Mindy went from a career as a clinical school social worker to a homeschool mom of four. Fast forward 19 years and now as a semi-sorta empty nester she is leaning into her passion for working with families as a certified life and grief coach and home school expert.

She firmly believes heart-centered parenting creates peace of mind and confidence for everyone in the family. Through empowering and equipping parents with tools and strategies to connect, communicate, and cope effectively, they can thrive.

She deeply desires for families to feel optimistic even in the midst of the transitions of life. It's her mission to help parents bring lightness, laughter, and love into their homes. With a good dose of humor and grace, she knows it is possible to live a life full of joy and love.

ELIANE LEPINE

NO LONGER A WALLFLOWER

Hey, beauty, my name is Eliane (pronounced Ellie-Ann) and a little over two years ago I decided to take my dreams seriously.

I had no idea where to start.

I felt unworthy of everything I desired.

I felt completely overwhelmed with the road ahead.

Does any of this sound familiar? Just like any purpose-driven woman, I had toyed with the idea of creating my dream life for a long time. In my case, that meant working from my laptop with my toes dug deep in the sand and mojito in hand. As I was approaching 30, feeling purposeless, I made a conscious decision to stop letting my life pass me by. This is the story of what finally triggered me to take back control of my life!

Fast forward to today, I'm quarantined in a tiny one-bedroom AirBnB apartment in Montreal with plans of traveling to San Diego canceled due to COVID-19. Even now, I've never felt as much freedom and fulfillment as I do at this moment. I'm finally living the life of purpose I knew I was meant for and know it's just a matter of time until I get to work poolside in the sun again.

The path to getting everything I desired was an unexpected and unpredictable one. *Remember how I said I had no idea where to start?* I knew about point A, (the situation I was desperately trying to get away from), and point B, freedom, baby! Yet the road to get there had no clear instructions and it felt overwhelming and scary.

At the time, I was working as an executive assistant for financial advisors. I'd been with the same company for three years, and I got along with everyone. My boss made me feel valued. I always got extended vacation time and would travel to my heart's content. I had the flexibility to make my hours in four days instead of five; this gave me time to finish my MBA. From the outside, it looked like I should've kept my head down and appreciated what I had, but I'd fall asleep at night with a niggling voice telling me I was meant for so much more. Still, I pushed on.

Never asked for help, instead, I took on work others couldn't finish (at work & school). I always said yes when my friends invited me to go out even if that meant canceling plans with myself or pushing the limits of my energy levels. I was trying to be and do it all for everyone else but myself.

In the background, anxiety was building up and depressed thoughts were flooding my brain. I had PTSD from a recent breakup that I was ignoring. Most of the friends that I was aiming to please were actually incompatible with my values and priorities. I was neglecting my mental and physical health on many levels. Instead, I was choosing to numb myself. It all felt pointless. I was spreading myself too thin and for what?

The more sad thoughts I experienced, the more I would go out with friends and take on more work and classes so I didn't have to face the disappointing parts of my life. What I needed was to pause and take an honest look at my life to reassess my priorities, but that felt way too scary. It was much easier to keep droning on.

The only thing that kept me hanging on was getting to work early and sitting in Starbucks while enjoying a sweet Cinnamon Almond Macchiato and watching replays of The Late Night Show for some giggles. Even going out with friends had lost its appeal. I'd come home after a happy hour feeling like I'd wasted my time and money. It's disconcerting when the people you rely on to elevate your mood just don't make you feel joyful anymore.

My life felt like it was approaching a dead end.

Thankfully, that little niggling voice kept poking me from different angles trying to get my attention. The thing that finally got me to pay attention was a thought so unsettling that it forced me to pause. I realized that every day I let go by without making a change, I was choosing to settle for a mediocre life.

Since when was I the kind of woman that settled?

My friends didn't fit my life. My job was slowly sucking the life out of me. I had no clear future goals. I was simply drifting along and accepted whatever life handed me. The thought of settling rattled me to my core. I had to fix it; I knew there was something better out there for me, but it didn't feel right to pursue it just yet.

I had dug myself into a deep dark hole where there was no room to have fun, no creativity allowed, and I was done living there. All I could think of was my younger self who loved to draw, dance, laugh, and create things. How sad she would be if she could see how her future self had turned out. She'd be angry with me for letting our life turn out this way. I needed something to get excited about again.

After leaving an abusive relationship, I sought validation through higher education. However, that wasn't cutting it anymore. Like many ambitious women, it was not in my nature to ask for help. I didn't even know how to. One Saturday afternoon I felt called to look at job posting sites, and I found an internship opportunity to learn online marketing with a startup company in the self-care industry.

For the first time in a very long time, I knew that applying for this internship was the right place to start. I'd learn new skills that could potentially help me find work online so I wouldn't be trapped in an office. I'd get guidance from someone who was building a company from the ground up. I felt like this was a project I could get excited about and learn a lot from the company's founder.

With every new beginning, hard decisions must be made. There would be a few things I would need to cut out to work for this startup. I had to keep my day job, so I decided to quit pursuing my MBA and to enforce better boundaries with my friends.

Seeing as most of these relationships weren't quality friendships, it felt great to take a step back. The thing that was hardest to let go of was school. I mourned my higher education for weeks and had to explain my choices to a few people around me who thought I'd gone mad.

Letting go of what I thought was valuable in exchange for my future was a challenge. However, every time I would meet with the startup CEO about a new product launch or how to improve our community, I felt like I was part of something that truly mattered. For the first time, I felt like I fit in; I'd finally found my people. That made me realize that a big part of feeling unworthy and undeserving of pursuing anything more than a mediocre life came from being aligned with the wrong people.

I thought I was weird for demanding more out of life, but that's because I didn't have the right support system. This showed me I could create my life however I wanted. I have a new rule: Never again dim my light or give up my desires for anyone in my life. I only want to surround myself with supportive individuals who see that light inside me and are always willing to celebrate it with me.

Learning to embrace my dreams and desires was a huge breakthrough for me about self-love. If you're reading this thinking, "I, too, also yield to the people in my life instead of honoring my passions," then the best thing I could say is to go find yourself a community to vibe with right now. No relationship is worth forgetting yourself, depriving the world of your unique gifts, or staying small.

If you know you're meant for something bigger, embrace it. Let that quiet voice inside you speak up. Let it know that it's entirely safe to feel what you feel and want what you want. Then start connecting with like-minded women ready to uplift you and inspire you to take back control of your future. Playing small is a vicious cycle that can only be broken with unconditional self-love.

I'll leave you with this: *If you're feeling stuck, overwhelmed, or unmotivated, are you putting everyone else's expectations above what you truly want? Or are you acting out of self-respect, self-love, and your own best interest?*

Learning to embrace my dreams and desires was a huge breakthrough for me about self-love. No relationship is worth forgetting yourself, depriving the world of your unique gifts, or staying small.

— ELIANE LEPINE

Eliane (pronounced Ellie-Ann) is a professional introvert, woo-woo loving, and latte obsessed marketing queen.

She deeply believes in the power of an embodied personal brand and picking just the right font to create the magnetizing success every woman wants for her business.

Her personal mission is to show women that feel stuck and unworthy exactly how to create financial freedom by honoring their true purpose and playing big.

With a little bit of the right strategy and a whole lot of unconditional self-love, she knows you can create the life you've always wanted.

OXANA ROMANYUK

SURVIVAL, REBIRTH, AND ULTIMATE SUCCESS

I'll begin with the imagery of the phoenix rising from the ashes as a symbol of rebirth and eternal life. A radiant bird, which near the end of its life, builds a pyre, bursts into flames, and then literally rises from its ashes. I went through a deeply emotional and spiritual change comparable to this metaphorical transformation before emerging with the radiance of independence, emotional health, and career success that many aspire to achieve.

My story of survival and rebirth starts on the coast of the Arctic Ocean, in the small fishing village of Krasnoshchelye, where I came into this world. I don't remember much about the village, except for a single picture snapped during my short reindeer ride from the birthing center. In it, you can see me wrapped in something affectionately known as a "deer envelope" because Russian winters are bone-chilling and the deerskin baby blanket was an absolute necessity.

As soon as I began my first baby steps, my family moved on from that small coastal village to an industrial city, Dzerzhinsk, not far from Moscow. As young medical professionals, my parents changed locations every two to three years. They were both members of the "Soviet Workforce Distribution Program" (*think "Doctors Without Borders" but...within the borders of Russia)*. My father was a nurse and my mother was a dentist, they found themselves whisked away to rural and remote places wherever medical help was needed. In hindsight, Dzerzhinsk would go on to become my family's permanent home but not before many, many more moves.

We traveled tremendous distances. A single train ride between towns, across the Soviet Union's vast expanse, would take up to six days of straight travel. I grew up on these trains. Those early memories of cross-country journeys planted a seed in me. They gave me a great love of Trans-Siberian travels and later, as an adult, fueled my passion for helping others with booking their own train adventures. But, that's later in the story.

I didn't know it at the time yet these early travel experiences in this formative period of my life, would teach me the value of survival. I learned quickly how to adapt to new routines and environments, how to build new friendships, how to navigate new relationships with classmates and school teachers every time we moved, and how to be resilient and independent. Handling stressful moving situations with the backdrop of the fall of the Soviet Union brought a lot of chaos, overwhelm, and uncertainty into my childhood.

I was seven years old when the collapse happened. Being so young, I could not fully grasp the concept: *the dissolution of the Soviet Union.* I remember standing in long lines with my parents to buy the most basic foods using rations and tear-off coupons. I also remember my friends with well-connected parents who had access to better quality, fresher produce, expensive clothing and electronics, novel and foreign drinks, and sweets like Chupa Chups, Juicy Fruit, Pepsi, and Snickers. My parents did not have connections so when we traveled, we always rented houses with a backyard that we used as a garden to grow our own fresh food to eat. We wore the same clothes continually and made do with what we had.

Something I remember vividly is that I was surrounded by an entire country of people just trying to *survive.* Following the Soviet collapse, the skyrocketing inflation caused millions of Russians to lose their savings and my family wasn't an exception. I clearly remember my mother and father in tears, anxious, and incredibly upset when they found out that their hard-earned money saved for a new house was wiped out, devalued, and worth nothing.

This wasn't the time for the privilege of lofty, philosophical questions, like: *"Who am I?"*, *"What is my place in the world?"* or *"Am I serving my life's purpose?"* The fall led to a mindset of *"silently doing what you were supposed to do."* While those questions would later occupy a lot of time in my mind, the average person was concerned with doing what they had to do to provide for their family and to keep their job at all costs.

It was a survival mentality that became ingrained in me. I began to form small, unrecognizable habits like being mindful of food leftovers, planning for a rainy day, never living on credit, mending my own clothes, relying on nature, and spending a lot of time outdoors, mushroom hunting, and berry gathering. I did what I had to do. I lived from a place of obligation to cultural concepts that I didn't question until I was older.

While keeping our heads low and doing what we had to do to survive as a family, I am mostly referring to our emotions and frustrations, having an open channel of communication, would have been tremendously helpful in coping with the daily overwhelming feelings I felt. However, my family never talked about that. We quickly dealt with problems and coped in our unique ways.

For me, I focused a lot on my studies and used good grades and achievements to win recognition and friendships. Believe me, this was not an easy task. The schooling system in Russia is different from that of the United States. Rather than children graduating from one level to another, Russian students are attached to the same classroom at school and teachers come to them at every grade level. The cohort that students start within kindergarten is the same one they graduate with. What that meant for me was that it was increasingly difficult to juggle constant moving with making new friends, especially in high school, and routinely inserting myself into cohorts where everyone had been friends for years.

In my senior year of high school, between sixteen and eighteen years old, Russian students choose their career path or trade. I had chosen the path of becoming an educator because I believe teaching to be a noble profession. I was accepted to a Russian pedagogical university and graduated with honors from the five-year program to be a teacher of English. I worked at an English private school in Russia while looking for a student exchange program that would allow me to travel to the United States to improve my English. I thought it would be an amazing achievement and a great privilege to study at an English-speaking university. Then I shifted from teaching back to being a student because I had to study long and hard to pass the English language proficiency exam required to attend an American university.

Looking back at my first few years of learning English, I would study from random books that my father brought home. I had such a naive hope and trust in him that learning English would be good for me. I studied diligently, even though, growing up, the English teachers kept leaving because they never seemed to want to settle in the rural places where I lived. I didn't blame them. I smile and shake my head at little Oxana, learning a foreign language with no idea how to pronounce and read the words correctly. Somehow it worked because I had two brilliant tutors later on and I successfully passed the English test which meant I was going to the grand U-S-of-A.

Arriving in the United States was an adventure in and of itself. I landed in Denver, Colorado. Why Denver and not Albuquerque, New Mexico, where the University was? I have no idea. I think the airplane tickets were somehow cheaper to fly into Denver. There I was with no cellphone and a map, trying to navigate my way by Greyhound bus to get to the University of New Mexico. I made it eventually, and after a period of intensely missing my family, cultural adaptation, and a remarkable amount of personal bravery, I graduated.

After completing my exchange year, I was accepted into a Master's program in Linguistics. In the same year that I had started the Master's program, I got married to my ex-husband. *Ex* being the spoiler that it didn't work out. We separated four years later. In addition to trying to rebuild my life after a divorce, I experienced the stigmatic shame of traditional Russian thinking. The shame came with the title of divorcée. Once a woman marries a man, it becomes her solemn duty to keep him at all costs. If the marriage ends in divorce, as it did for me, then it's seen as the woman's fault: *Something must be wrong with her, or she must have done something for him to leave.* After officially getting divorced, even though it was amicable, I thought my life and prospects were over. I felt as though I had failed as a woman in some way because I couldn't *keep my man* and culturally speaking, *I was damaged goods*. I thought to myself: *Who would want me now?*

As it turns out, a beautiful and intelligent woman named Patrice did. I had had a girl crush on her practically since we met. I was captivated by the way she carried and expressed herself. She's eloquent, ambitious, and charismatic. I was shy and nervous to make my interest and intentions known. Many of Patrice's friends had warned her not to get too close to me and not to take things too seriously between us for fear that I would hop to the next relationship, most likely with a man. Despite this, we began dating, and it was chivalrous how she asked me to go on a date.

She sat me down on the couch and said, "Oxana Romanyuk, would you like to date me?"

I felt seen, loved, and cared for at that moment. To this day, it makes me giddy to think about it. Life wasn't all chivalry and smiles, however, as I had mixed support from my family and my father and sister were strongly against my life partner choice. In addition to the new relationship uncertainties, I also felt the shame of being a career-hopper, which is another *no-no* in Russian thinking.

I hopped from being an English teacher in Russia to tutoring Russian and teaching English at UNM, to being a Russian instructor for military linguists, and then to working at a leisure travel agency for five years. I wasn't following the classic Russian path of picking a career and sticking with it. My mother and father were with their jobs for thirty years. My sister is fanatically devoted to her career, and my brother has been working in his business for decades. The traditional expectation of everyone holding onto their jobs fiercely was born during the collapse of the Soviet Union. The continuity of the same job provided a sense of stability. Although the economic uncertainties were alleviated by the 2000s, within my family, the status-quo remained. I was the odd one out for hopping about, and I internalized this feeling of being out of place. I often felt judged and unsafe to fully share with my parents everything that was happening in my life. After many years of habitually burying my feelings alive, I had a huge iceberg-level of emotions looming under the surface that could have sunk the Titanic. That's how the beginning of 2014 felt for me.

I began the year in Washington, DC. Around me, hope, resolutions, and fireworks filled the air. Everyone was bustling with visions of what they would achieve and who they would become, everyone, that is, except me. For me, I felt stuck, bored, unmotivated, and burnt out. It was the kind of burnt out that left life feeling like a sticky mess. A mess of unfamiliar, uncomfortable, and unpleasant feelings. Unresolved emotions were consuming me and transforming me into a blob of a human being. However, I didn't know which tools I needed to help me feel better.

I didn't set any goals, and I wasn't sure what the year would bring. Little did I know that 2014 would be a big year of change and growth for me. I was moments away from a breakdown that would ultimately catapult me in the direction of success on my terms, three years later. Something had to change, and it needed to change fast. I was walking a path of defying traditional Russian expectations, drowning in a sea of emotions that had me questioning my life and life's purpose. I slowly came to recognize that this a quarter-life crisis in some senses and it reeked of privilege. You have to be at a point where you can contemplate more than basic survival, or just how to make ends meet to have the capacity to examine your position in the world. I had reached this point. At the time, I was working as a senior destination specialist for a leisure travel agency. My job was to sell tours and cruises to Russia, Europe, and Eastern European countries. I had one of the highest salaries for my position because I was good at my job. By external measurements, I was successful. I had studied hard, worked hard, and had a good job. I was doing what I was supposed to do. *So what was the problem?*

At first, I lived vicariously through my sales. I loved working with eager, adventurous, curious, and excited travelers. I loved hearing their enthusiasm on the phone and loved getting to know them, their travel interests, and their inspirations. I made their travel dreams come true with the utmost quality, dedication, professionalism, and warmth. Building relationships and friendships with our customers brought me a lot of joy. I became a part of the customer's story, like a fairy godmother waving a magic wand behind the scenes to make their travel dreams a reality.

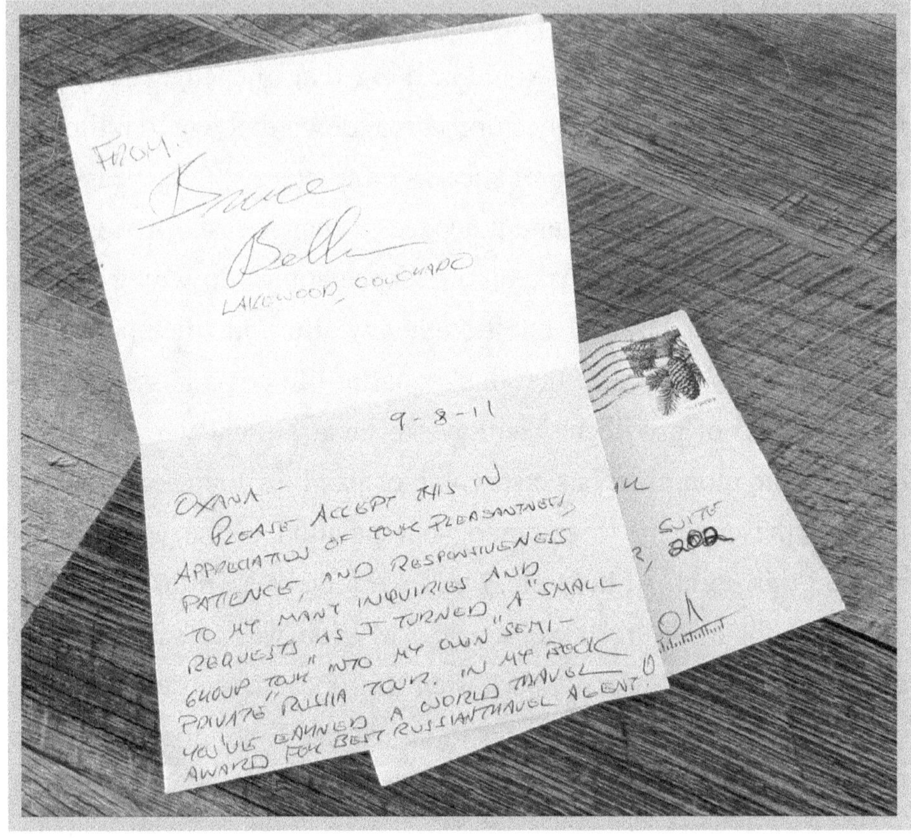

After about three years, however, the sales race and quotas began to take a toll on me, and I wanted to expand my degree of influence within the company. I had a few ideas about how I could apply my knowledge and expertise to other departments. I approached management and initiated several conversations about my career growth and professional development. I explained that I wanted to start transitioning from sales to using my valuable experience in training new team members, product development, and building corporate partnerships. Unfortunately, the only plan the company had for me was to stay where I was and to keep generating steady sales. After unsuccessful attempts to carve out a new path to grow and create more impact within the company, I started feeling unheard, unseen, depleted, and anxious. I had hit my ceiling. Our team faced constant pressure to perform at our best, and the sales quotas were rising, and as were my stress levels.

I am very competitive, and being the last in sales was out of the question. I forced myself to perform, put a smile on my face, sounded enthusiastic and excited on the phone, and succeeded at crossing things off of my to-do list with vigor. On the surface, I did this to be able to say that I was the first one to finish all my follow-up calls for the day. Underneath this, though, I was doing what I had always done which was pushing myself towards excellence to resolve those sticky emotions that I kept trying to bury. However, it wasn't working, and my love tank was getting extremely low.

My love languages are acts of service and quality time, and, at first, this job was perfect for both because I loved being of service and taking care of our clients. I agonized over every little detail, especially when it came to the most complex of itineraries. Undoubtedly, Trans-Siberian railway adventures, which took between 15 to 28 days, were my most favorite, logistically challenging trips to plan. My eyes lit up and my heart smiled every time a traveler told me they were interested in taking a train tour. I used every chance I got to tell them my childhood stories about our train travels and tried to ease their concerns about the logistics and the remote places they were about to visit. Many things could go wrong in the execution of these intricate routes; that's why, I always selected and booked the best guides, drivers, hotels, transportation, and destinations. I imagined myself as a traveler and did for them what I would want others to do for me.

To this day, I remember many of my clients vividly. One of the most memorable moments was getting an email from a Colonel who was serving in Pakistan. He had minimal internet access, and his emails arrived split into several different messages. The story, though, was sweet.

He said, "I miss my fiance. I haven't seen her in a year and a half, and I want to plan a secret trip where we meet up for a cruise in Russia."

The meetup must have been like something from a movie. I booked them the most romantic cruise of their dreams. It was a new five-star cruise ship that was incomparable in its class. I was excited that he chose this particular experience. I knew that there was guaranteed to be a high level of service, comfort, and the type of itinerary that would make memories that would last a lifetime.

He wanted her to be surprised, and I wanted them both to have an unforgettable experience together, therefore, I booked surprises for them of my own. I booked them one of the higher-category cabins. Then negotiated an upgrade with the cruise director to a honeymoon suite that was also one of the largest staterooms aboard the ship. I also planned a private surprise dinner for them, after hours, in one of the palaces in St. Petersburg. My client reached back out to me again once he was back on the base. He sent me a gift box with a sweet note and a beautiful pashmina (a traditional woven scarf made of wool and silk). I still have it with me in my closet to this day, it was such a precious gift to me. The note said how great their trip was, how they were able to reconnect, and how they had a fantastic experience. Honestly, my heart melted from his feedback on his emails and then melted again with the gift that I received. It touched me deeply that I was able to create this exceptional experience for them and play a small role in their romantic reconnection.

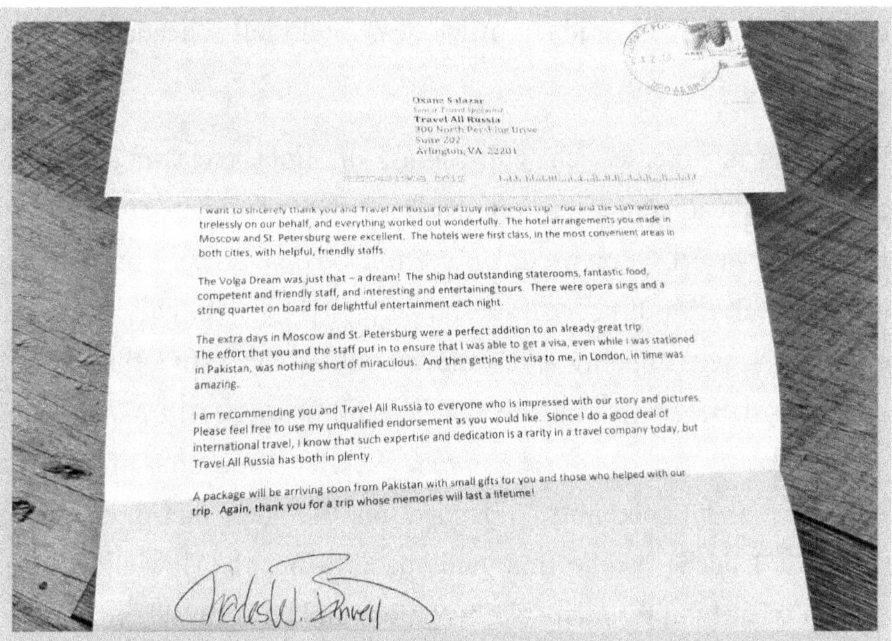

Oxana Salazar
Senior Travel Specialist
Travel All Russia
300 North Pershing Drive
Suite 202
Arlington, VA 22201

I want to sincerely thank you and Travel All Russia for a truly marvelous trip! You and the staff worked tirelessly on our behalf, and everything worked out wonderfully. The hotel arrangements you made in Moscow and St. Petersburg were excellent. The hotels were first class, in the most convenient areas in both cities, with helpful, friendly staffs.

The Volga Dream was just that – a dream! The ship had outstanding staterooms, fantastic food, competent and friendly staff, and interesting and entertaining tours. There were opera sings and a string quartet on board for delightful entertainment each night.

The extra days in Moscow and St. Petersburg were a perfect addition to an already great trip. The effort that you and the staff put in to ensure that I was able to get a visa, even while I was stationed in Pakistan, was nothing short of miraculous. And then getting the visa to me, in London, in time was amazing.

I am recommending you and Travel All Russia to everyone who is impressed with our story and pictures. Please feel free to use my unqualified endorsement as you would like. Sionce I do a good deal of international travel, I know that such expertise and dedication is a rarity in a travel company today, but Travel All Russia has both in plenty.

A package will be arriving soon from Pakistan with small gifts for you and those who helped with our trip. Again, thank you for a trip whose memories will last a lifetime!

My positive experiences at work, however, were dwindling. Work stopped bringing me joy and instead brought me emotional and physical exhaustion from the stress and pressure of sales. I went from being the nurturing and caring travel agent, who was deeply committed to creating unforgettable travel experiences, to a withdrawn, drained, and indifferent employee. I was ready to get up and leave for good any second, and that's exactly what ended up happening. One day, smack in the middle of the workweek, right around lunch, I had a meeting with my manager in which we discussed both team and individual sales numbers and performance. My ticking bomb of dissatisfaction, unhappiness, and fatigue exploded. I got up, said I couldn't do it anymore, exited the conference room, cleared my office desk, and I left. I headed home to have a glass of wine.

Sitting on my Ikea couch with a glass of Rioja, red wine, I deeply exhaled. I breathed out tension, disappointment, anxiety, and years of not being heard, supported, or seen. Don't get me wrong, I was scared. I felt lost, directionless, and surprised by what had happened, yet also I felt hopeful and relieved all at the same time. Then suddenly, I began to imagine the possibilities, and *started to think about what it was I wanted for myself.* After some time of swirling emotions and uncertainty, I landed on the idea that I needed a getaway. I needed some time and space to breathe. I would do for myself what I did for many clients before and book myself a trip.

I thought back to my experience of a friend introducing me to a spiritual person named Amma (Mātā Amritānandamayī Devī). What

Amma is known for is hugging and loving people unconditionally, traveling the world, and giving spiritual talks about kindness and compassion. My friend invited me to see her, as she just so happened to be on tour, and was giving a talk at a hotel in DC. I listened to Amma's spiritual messages, participated in the devotional singing, and witnessed her endlessly and lovingly hugging everyone who showed up. I also got a token, lined up along with everyone else, and just waited for my hug.

I came up on stage to receive her embrace. It was a truly remarkable experience. That hug, I still remember every second of it, every emotion I felt in the moment, every motion I went through to end up in her loving arms. It felt so comforting and so motherly. There was so much warmth and kindness in that hug. Afterward, as I was talking to the program organizers, I learned that Amma owned an ashram, a holy place, in the south of India, where she built out a monastery open to Indians and westerners alike.

Local and foreign visitors stay at Amma's ashram for as long as they wish: pay for lodging, practice yoga and meditation, do soul searching, take silent retreats, and volunteer. *I decided that was where I needed to go.* I needed to find that feeling again, to connect beyond myself, to feel reassured, to know I had a purpose. I planned a solo trip to travel through India and stay at the ashram for as long as I needed it. I had the naive notion, thanks to the media and movies like "Eat. Pray. Love.", that exploring India was going to be part of this grand journey of finding myself and discovering my place in the world. India, in my mind at the time, was known for being a place of spiritual awakening, of connecting with destiny. I was ready. I had sold most of my belongings and had put the rest in storage. I set out with a clean slate, encouragement from Patrice, and a willingness to just receive.

With my private guides and drivers, I thoroughly explored Delhi and discovered India's golden triangle, which connects Delhi, Agra, and Jaipur. I finished my adventure in South India, in a small coastal fishing village of Parayakadavu. Amma's ashram was my home for two months. I spent my days attending fire pujas every morning, doing rooftop yoga and mediation, volunteering, and helping Russian-speaking visitors with translations and acclimatization. I also practiced singing in a Russian choir, which had the honor of performing for Amma right before my departure.

Contrary to my vision and hope, by the end of my experience in India, I still didn't know what I wanted to do next. I was basking in the feelings of new adventures, discoveries, new friendships, and cultural experiences. I returned to DC distracted, but disappointed that I didn't suddenly have all of the answers. Add to this that I had a layer of culture shock, going from the calm, peaceful, meditative environment of the ashram to the noise, hustle, and bustle of DC. I found myself quickly experiencing all of those sticky emotions again. My mind wrestled with the near impossibility of reconciling the fact that I could have sustained myself for an entire year in India with just one month's rent living in DC. Readjusting took a couple of months.

I didn't know what I wanted to do with my life, but I did know that I had to make a change. Along with my spiritual journey, I decided to change my lifestyle. I became a vegetarian. I cut out alcohol and dove deeper into yoga and meditation. My lifestyle changes also brought about an overhaul of my social circle because I was transforming into a different person from who I was. It was a slow natural progression with my friends first being unable to relate to my soul-searching experiences, then giving me space *to go figure things out*, and finally *forgetting* to invite me to their gatherings, events, and parties. Just like that, in a year, I lost most of my trusted friends.

I was examining my thoughts, desires, and feelings at a deeper level and sought to add more meaning to my life. I tried working in a DC non-profit organization where I felt my work was purposeful and valuable. However, financially I wasn't able to sustain myself. The struggle of internal conflict was real. I wanted to feel that my work was important and rewarding, but I was still clinging, at least in part, to the side of myself that believed my worth was tied to how much money I made. Unable to reconcile the financial reality and my desire for greater meaning at this point in my journey, my career hopping continued.

I decided to return to the travel industry; only this time, I chose to work with the corporate travelers. It wasn't long at all before I began to experience signs in my body that this career path wasn't for me. With the high demands and expectations of the VIP travelers, stress and lack of appreciation within the job combined with the corporate culture of wining and dining weren't working for me. I began having heart palpitations from the stress and had to choose between a lucrative job or my health. Needless to say, I was relieved to leave the position. The health risks of a high-stress lifestyle weren't worth it to me. I found myself once again *questioning my path and what I should do*. More than ever, I was struggling with my identity being tied up in the capitalist mindset of my self-worth being associated with the amount of money that I made.

By 2017, I was feeling completely and utterly purposeless when it came to my career path. I was so lost. I had tried the non-profit route, and while I found meaning in it, I was unable to sustain myself financially, and I had tried the corporate track, which nourished my wallet but not my body or soul. *I didn't know what I was doing with my life.* I was hopping from career-path to career-path. I was searching for my purpose in the world. *If I wasn't of use, then what kind of life was I living?* Some people have this experience of looking out at the night sky and feeling small and insignificant when faced with the vast expansiveness of the universe. I had internalized this feeling of insignificance such that I had an empty void inside me. *How could I reconcile my need for contribution and meaning within a career with the financial reality that almost everything in life costs something?* Shelter, food, entertainment, hobbies, and traveling by any other modality than walking, everything could be turned into a calculation of how much money is required. It felt bleak, as though my existence was epitomized in dollar bills floating away.

I felt the lowest of the low. If I was burnt out in 2014, I was nothing but a pile of ashes in 2017. I had been soul searching to the depths of my being for three arduous years, and I was feeling a mounting internal pressure that I should have *made it* by now, that I should have been successful or had everything figured out already. My internal timeline of *should-haves* wasn't aligning with my reality, year after year. Luckily for me, though, this is a phoenix story, so there is a silver lining. This burnt out, fed-up position, was priming me for a new beginning. I was so close to discovering my path, my calling, my niche, and I had no idea.

I returned to my career hopscotch pattern and began working at a local DC yoga studio part-time. I gained valuable skills and insights while improving my health and wellness. At the same time, I offered administrative services online and started to enjoy the freedom and flexibility of my virtual work provided. I can easily say that yoga, selfless service, meditation, and virtual assistant work was a winning combination for me. Connecting my mind, body, and soul in yoga, performing spiritual practices, starting to generate additional revenue while serving virtual clients, feeling needed, and in-demand pulled me out of the darkness I had been in for so long. In being able to offer my services online and location independent, I saw an opportunity to fulfill a great need within the industry in a way that matched my core values. Not only this, but it had opened my eyes to a transformative way of thinking about the deep-seated obligations that I had felt. That was it. That was my big turning point.

After years of spiritual journeying and completing yoga teacher training, I had finally turned inward and decided that I mattered, that what I had to offer the world was valuable. My mind had expanded because of the awareness and presence that I had cultivated, and I began to recognize my truth, that I am the creator of my own reality.

At that point, I leaped and founded my own business, Remote Rockstars®. I had been waiting for the answers and searching for some external validation. I had deeply wanted some outward sign that *this* or *that* was what I was meant to do in the world, who I was intended to become. I had done all that I could think to have done, but it wasn't until I started to live life according to my internal convictions and values that I began to walk my true path. I slowly moved from struggling with all of those sticky emotions to a path of wellness. I devoted more time to expanding my spiritual and internal world. I began listening to my feelings and my body. I carved out more space for myself within myself. It was a life-changing experience when I decided to live out who I truly am at the core of my being. I was able to assess and to overcome the limiting beliefs that I was harboring in terms of my identity and self-worth.

My eyes were opened to the idea that I didn't have to be a corporate sellout to be successful; meaning that I didn't have to exchange my values for a sizable paycheck. As my own boss, I could have my cake and eat it too. For me, that meant that I could create a business infused with my limitless potential and core values: compassion, honesty, integrity, and courage. This notion brought my soul a lot of freedom. I began to dream again: *What would it look like to start my own business? How would I do things differently? What would my company culture inspire?* Like that moment of leaving the leisure travel agency and coming home to a glass of wine, new possibilities opened up in my mind.

I quickly decided that integrity was a must because my core values centered on treating everyone with love, compassion, and kindness. Being honest is truly the best policy. Then combining honesty, transparency, and confidentiality is critical for all of my business interactions. As is a habit, I imagine myself as one of my clients and consider the experience of being on the other side of the computer screen. *How would I want to feel as a client? What would be my core concerns?*

Thinking through and agonizing over every detail, similar to those complicated train itineraries I used to design, provided me a lot of insight into what I want for my clients and what they would want from my business. Similarly, I thought through the experience that I wanted to create for my team members. I decided that my company culture would be family-oriented and my business would be personal to me, in the truest sense. Teammates would genuinely care about one another, and everyone would abide by the laws of mutual kindness and respect. While I was figuratively a pile of ashes in 2017, I was on a new path entirely by the following year.

In 2018, I was the phoenix reborn, ready to expand my wings and my business. I began looking for subcontractors. I had a greater vision of purpose and direction. I had always been willing to roll up my sleeves and put in the hard work, but I just needed to know what it was that I was working hard to build, and I needed the big picture to align with my internal values. With this newfound clarity and direction, I also got married to Patrice. She stood by me through all of my soul-searching and uncertainty, and I knew I wanted to continue to build my future with her in it. With these milestones, life began to take on an entirely different vibe. Although starting a business comes with a lot of precariousness, by 2019, I had solidified my team and client-base, and by 2020 was able to dream of new horizons upon which to soar.

Having been born in a small fishing village in Russia, growing up amid the backdrop of the USSR collapse, and then making it to become a successful entrepreneur in the United States of America, was such a thorn-filled experience. However, my upbringing, with all of its bittersweet moments, primed me to be the person that I am today. I learned to be nurturing and dependable from taking care of my family members during times of struggle. I climbed the corporate ladder of *success*, first according to what I had been raised to believe about the world, and then second, I climbed it based on values that I established for myself.

Central to my experiences is the need to live out a life of contribution. Thinking back upon when I was unhappy, those were the moments that I struggled the most to connect my actions to meaningful contributions in the lives of others. When sales became about the numbers, the ability to lead a life of contribution waned because the emphasis turned from *how can I provide the most value in the lives of the customers?* to *how can they provide the most value to me?*

That's why the work that I do today brings me so much satisfaction and joy because I can focus on providing meaning to others. It speaks directly to my love languages and my need to be of service. Part of the beauty of volunteering at Amma's ashram was the silence behind *seva* or selfless service. There was an enrichment of connecting one's actions to the work being done. It allowed for increased devotion without unnecessary distractions from the internal goals of the self. Honing in on that level of focus or dedication to the task at hand proved invaluable for me and the way that I am now able to connect meaningfully with my role in my business. I can tap into that same selfless dedication and apply it to creating value that ripples beyond the lives of my customers.

Remote Rockstars® directly and indirectly, facilitates significant growth opportunities within companies and communities. By leveraging my company's valuable virtual assistance and online business management, six and seven-figure entrepreneurs can prioritize new visions and directions for their organizations. Additionally, their reclaimed time is free to be invested in their families, which promotes healthier lifestyles and happier communities.

Especially in light of the recent challenges in the world, in which the job market is seeing great fluctuations and shifts in day-to-day operations, now, more than ever, the professional skills and virtual services that my business, Remote Rockstars®, offers is something of significant value. It's such an honor for me to know that I am part of the group of virtual professionals in the world who can offer jobs and that sense of security many individuals seek following periods of economic uncertainty.

It blows my mind and brings me a lot of joy that I was able to persevere through the bitter stages of life and not allow those sticky emotions to limit me forever. Now, I appreciate with an even greater depth the sweetness of life. While our team continues to grow and we look forward to expansive possibilities for the future, I wanted to leave you with a parting note, our team's word for the year 2020: *elevate*. Or in other words, *rise*, just like a phoenix.

This burnt out, fed-up position, was priming me for a new beginning. I was so close to discovering my path, my calling, my niche, and I had no idea.

— OXANA ROMANYUK

Oxana Romanyuk is the founder and CEO of Remote Rockstars® that offers high-end online business management and professional virtual assistant services to visionary entrepreneurs, industry experts, and coaches. Oxana works with her home-grown team of rockstar account managers and virtual assistants, helping entrepreneurs systematize and grow their businesses.

Oxana is a certified Online Business Manager and a proud member of the International Association of Online Business Managers and Association of Virtual Assistants.

She's trained countless virtual assistants and has helped multiple entrepreneurs grow their businesses, reach more people, and impact the world.

Socials:

Facebook: Remote Rock Stars

Facebook: Remote Rock Stars Club

Instagram: Remote Rock Stars

LITA VALLIS

DEATH BY PERFECTIONISM

This is my third grade self talking to my mother who was lovingly putting my hair up in ponytails before school...for the third time in the morning. "There are still bumps!" I exclaimed as if having bumps on the sides of my head where the hair pulled back over my ears was the absolute end of the world and my reputation as a third-grade hairstyle fashionista. No Bumps.

PART I: THE EARLY YEARS

"There are bumps! Do it over!"

It must be perfectly smooth. That was my rule. My mother indulged me, usually for longer than I thought she would, re-doing my hair three, four, even sometimes five times every morning before school.

Then my mom will say something along the lines of, "That's it. That is the best I can do. You are going to be late for school. Now go eat your breakfast. Your hair looks fine."

She pronounced as her final, exasperated plea to be released from her hairdresser duties to a high maintenance 8-year-old girl. I sullenly gave up on reaching my pinnacle of perfectly smooth hair as I sighed deeply, wrought with my exasperation, slowly getting down off the chair to go eat breakfast and finish getting ready for school. This is my earliest memory of what would become my lifelong struggle with perfectionism.

Flash forward a couple of years. My childhood pièce de résistance was my fifth-grade language arts class where we were assigned a poetry project. We each had to write one of each type of poem including metaphor, simile, onomatopoeia, acrostic, haiku, and more. I was in my element. The assignment itself opened up new pathways of creativity in my young brain and ideas began flowing effortlessly from my joyful mind. I was writing constantly from that point on, thinking of new ideas for each of the categories. Often while doing the work, pens, and colored pencils were flying, this did not even feel like schoolwork. This was my first experience of heaven on earth. I fell in love with writing poetry and experienced my first complete flow state for about a month leading up to the due date of that poetry project. Then came the deadline and the name itself implies...death. It was the death of my flow. My joy around the project quickly came to a halt as I started having to put the pages together and type up the final draft, add a cover page, illustrations, and hand in the project to be graded. Graded. My art would be graded. It was not something I was looking forward to and certainly did not inspire my creativity. My world was altered forever. My words were going to be judged. My creativity came to a screeching halt as I realized that my art would be critiqued by my teacher and it meant something bad if they did not like it. It could mean something was bad about me. I was so passionate about this newly discovered art form, I could not bear the thought of my poems possibly not being good enough to earn her approval. I might not be good enough.

Things devolved quickly around my house the week of the fateful poetry project deadline. My loving mom began her duty of nagging me.

She would say, "Have you finished your project? It's due on Friday."

I would say, " I know, I know. Leave me alone,"

Or I mumbled under my breath, "Ugh."

I found many creative ways to procrastinate that week. The week quickly went by, Tuesday came and went, then Wednesday, and now Thursday. My mom was exasperated and finally, she said she was going to sit down with me and guard me until I finished the project. We were up all night assembling my poems into a readable and organized form. It was one of the worst nights in my illustrious seven-year academic history. My mom was furious and grumpy, and rightly so as the clock passed the 2 a.m. mark. We were both barely awake in front of our family typewriter.

My mom asked through her half-closed eyelids with a grumbly voice after staying up all night, "I don't understand why you waited until the last minute! Your poems are so lovely. Why wouldn't you get them ready earlier this week?"

I replied, "I don't know."

This was my only answer and it was the truth. I did not know why I felt paralyzed by finishing the project at the time. I knew that I did not want to hand in those poems to be graded, to be judged, and to be assessed by others. The writing process itself was so rewarding that to have them graded seemed so horrifying I simply could not bring myself to finish it. I didn't know the name of my affliction then, but I do now. This was my early confrontation with Perfectionism.

The Friday morning the project was due was fraught with conflict for me. So much so that I held onto these precious pages of poetry over the weekend. I kept reading them over again, hidden away in my room, wondering if they would be well received and bring my teacher as much joy as their creation brought me. These works of my soul needed to be set free, but I was not yet ready to bear the burden of another's pronouncement of their worth. They were still only mine, and they were still full of my untainted joy, at least until Monday.

When I finally turned in the project during English class that Monday morning, my teacher was pleased but made sure to let me know that I would not get an A because I had turned the assignment in late. I understood, and in a way, I was relieved. Now I would have an excuse to explain why my grade was sub-par. My work was tardy. It seemed less personal than my concern that maybe these poems were not as lovely or imaginative as I had experienced them to be during the process. I was fine with a lower grade for some other reason, like tardiness, that it did not relate to the intrinsic worth of these verbal expressions of my soul.

The next week as our projects were returned to us, my teacher went nuts over my poems. She told me I had great talent and encouraged me to continue by submitting my work to local contests and organizations for young poets. I remember basking in her praise as she was one of my favorite teachers, yet I was still resistant to this idea of contests, prizes, and "winners" within this art form. The same art form I recently discovered brought me a lot of joy. These prizes and contests implied there were indeed losers. Losers at poetry. Losers at art. It made no sense to me. I got an A-minus on the project, and I was fine with that, relieved actually.

That month I spent creating my fifth-grade poetry project was one of the last memories I have of free, unselfconscious creative flow. I did continue to write, yet all the memories I can recall later on during this time are tainted with self-criticism, self-consciousness, and fear of others' judgment. I didn't want to be a loser. I didn't want to be judged.

As this struggle plagued me into my teens and 20s, if it did not stop me from creating altogether, it kept me from sharing my work with others. I have countless journals filled with my original work yet this chapter that you are reading right now is only the second piece of writing I have published in over 30 years.

Perfectionism killed my youthful passion. My negative thoughts murdered my unbounded creativity. I imprisoned myself with my own death sentence: Death by Perfectionism. It started young and has stayed with me for decades. I have served a life sentence.

"What will they think?"

"It needs more work."

"Oh never mind, don't bother."

"Somebody else is already doing that anyway."

"You are not that good."

"Leave it to the professionals."

"You will never make any money at that."

"Your ideas are not original."

"You are too old to start now."

"There are a million writers in the world."

"You think you are some sort of influencer? Doesn't everyone? Get over yourself."

· · ·

The list goes on of things I have said to myself over the years to keep me from producing anything complete enough to share, sharing anything unfinished, or anything at all. Perfectionism has been the ultimate weapon for procrastination, self-sabotage, and keeping myself small. Sometimes I wielded my perfectionism so successfully that I convinced myself I didn't have any great passions at all. I lied to myself. I believed that lie. It was easier than dealing with the pain and sorrow of my perceived failure before I even began. I distracted myself with work, dating, partying, serving others' dreams, and ultimately living my life less to the fullest.

That voice inside my head that only speaks of lack, of imperfection, and speaks to the part of whatever I am doing that is wrong, bad, not good enough is always there. It was like a mean friend that wouldn't leave me alone but never helped me do anything productive. She just criticizes, yet I had gotten so used to her presence that she never got told to go home. She never left, and I never kicked her out. She just lingered…like a bad, noisy houseguest that stayed way too long.

She is a murderer. That may seem extreme, but she is a cause of death. She caused the death of my creativity, the death of my desire, the death of my passion, my playfulness, my sense of self-worth, and mainly, the death of my deepest purpose to share myself in a positive, powerful, and intimate way with others who may benefit from my contribution.

Some would call her a codependent, abusive, judgemental, narcissistic, mean girl. Some would call her other names. For the sake of this chapter, I will call her **MG**, Mean Girl. The mean girl for me is ever-present. My goal throughout my life thus far has been to deal with her in the best possible way, because **MG** is part of the human condition for many of us. Ignoring her never worked. She is very patient. She would often just wait until I thought she was gone and then whisper her messages into the back of my brain in such a subtle way that I would once again confuse her voice with my own.

Getting mad at her never worked either. She is one tough cookie. She can take a lot of anger and turn it into her own fuel to chew me down further.

She would say, "See how angry you get? You are not ready to deal with your issues. You should take another course. Or maybe go see a therapist. *Then maybe* you will be able to produce something of value to society. Just wait until you are really ready."

That day would never come if I kept listening to her.

Meditation has been the most effective tool I have found to silence **MG**. She still creeps into my space but at least now she feels *very very* uncomfortable here. I am building a life without her crippling influence. She may never go away, but over the years she has become easier to muffle...at least long enough to get out a few words...or in this case 4000 words as written here for this chapter. This chapter being published is in itself a testament to my relatively newfound freedom from her bitchy influence. I can't say that I finally kicked her out because she still lives with me. I can say that I moved her into the garage and now I only allow her in my mental house for very short periods. She comes in unannounced therefore I have to remind her that she is not welcome here. I have reclaimed my mental home as my sovereign domain. **MG** occasionally needs a reminder to go back to her garage, but she eventually gets the message and gets out of my way. I don't have room for her anymore.

This book project has been an exercise in overcoming my perfectionism. As I sit and write this copy, **MG** is still here, trying to sit next to me, telling me that the only reason I can get this out of my head and onto the page is the fact that she can go back and edit it later, making it better than it probably is right now. That is the only way I can type out this draft is by labeling it a draft, an incomplete, unfinished, soon-to-be-reworked draft because it is surely not good enough as it is without more work. It will all need to be reworked. Maybe it will. The difference is that now, after many years of self-reflection, I can laugh at **MG**. I can push her aside, send her back to the garage, dismiss her as the bully that she is, only here to interfere with my fun on the playground of life. I can work around her.

I have made a new friend on the playground. Her name is **DG**, Determined Girl, and she knows how to stay focused on what matters to me. She is my chosen playmate on this journey, and she supports my process of creation with encouragement and kindness. She focuses on the contribution and outcome we are creating without stopping and considering all of **MG's** snarky comments. She does not care as much about what others think, and she has declared war on **MG**. She has my best interests in mind, and I *love* hanging out with her. She is also here with me as I write this chapter, and she is full of wisdom and enthusiasm. We are new besties. She has moved into my mental house full time, and we are excellent roommates.

PART II: INNER CHILD HEALED

We are all natural creators in our own mediums. We are designed to create, to build, to flow, and to share our creative gifts with others. Whether it be in our relationships, our jobs, our homes, our art, or in noticing the natural world around us, we are part of this big, beautiful world and thus, we too are designed to create, grow, and express ourselves.

Let's consider nature directly for a moment. Is nature perfect or imperfect? Do we call a tree branch imperfect because it is too knotty? What if the branches curve one way and not another? If a branch breaks off, do we condemn the entire tree because it is now broken and imperfect? Why would we not consider ourselves and our own bodies, our own art, our own creations in the same way? Sometimes true beauty is found in the imperfection, the uniqueness, the so-called flaws that make us each one of a kind.

The Japanese art form of *Kintsugi* embodies this truth beautifully. When a vase cracks, it is glued back together with golden glue and is now considered more beautiful. The repair is now a part of the history of the object, adding to its uniqueness rather than something to cover or disguise. I think of this art form when I enjoy the wrinkles that are forming on my own face. The cracks forming around my eyes, earned by years of laughter, sometimes with many tears, just like the golden glue on the vase. I wear my crevasses with pride and know they make my face more unique and original. While many people get facelifts and botox (no judgment here), I would currently rather celebrate these changes as signs of a life well-lived. They are part of my history now. *Kintsugi.*

I like to think of creativity like clouds floating across the sky. As they continuously shift and morph, there is no perfect cloud shape. They are in constant flux, continuously awe-inspiring as they float by. If I tried to select the "perfect" cloud, I would be severely disappointed as it quickly morphed into a new shape, leaving the fantasy of perfection behind. Plus the fact that every person would have a different idea of what the perfect cloud would look like, hence it is a useless inquiry. Such as it is with the perfect song, the perfect voice, the perfect story, the perfect body, the perfect house, or the perfect life. *There is no such thing. It is all made up.* It only becomes real when we choose to believe it for ourselves and take it on like it's the truth.

"The woods would be very silent if no birds sang except those who sang best." Henry Van Dyke said this and truer words were never spoken. The world needs all kinds of birds to share their songs. I encourage you to share your voice, your song, your story, your life in whatever way inspires your passion and creativity. You are a unique contribution and there is someone out there who needs to hear your story as only you can share it.

That is my prayer for this writing, this chapter, and this book. May there be one less perfectionist in the world, and one more happily productive, creative human realizing that your uniqueness is the greatest gift you can give to others. There is no shame in sharing something that is "imperfect." When you are beginning, developing, or growing, the unfolding can be quite beautiful to witness. Please begin that great novel. Begin that poem, song, story, book, or script. Begin that home project, fashion design sewing project, new relationship, piano lessons, watercolor classes, or whatever it is you feel excited to begin or begin again. You may or may not receive accolades from others or approval from so-called experts in the field. You may not even get a dozen "likes" or "follows" if you post about it on social media, but you will receive the gift within yourself of fulfilling your natural purpose as a creator. You will receive fulfillment in the process of creation. When you are fulfilling yourself, you will most likely inspire others around you to fulfill their own visions and dreams. Whether or not you become a big sensation, gain a following, or become an "influencer", or win some made-up award, it doesn't matter. There are no winners at creation, and there are no losers. That is a made-up system, designed to keep us comparing and competing with others.

What If

What if we did everything we enjoy, simply for the sake of doing it? Creativity for the sake of being creative, singing for the sake of singing, playing for the sake of playing, process, and practice *as the art form in and of itself* with no destination or goal whatsoever?

Creativity this year has been a new experience of freedom. Freedom from being stopped by self-criticism, freedom from being controlled by procrastination and fear; freedom from all the complex facets of perfectionism. I write this chapter to share the journey in hopes that you, my reader, will learn from my years of wasted energy and move forward with your own creative endeavors with a renewed freedom. In this age of inundation of social media, stories, posts, shares, podcasts, vodcasts, vlogs, blogs, channels, and platforms with endless streams of content from billions of people around the world at our fingertips. I ask you, *why wouldn't you* share yours? If someone doesn't like what you are offering or sharing, they can simply turn the page, click elsewhere, or move on. *No big deal.*

Everyone is so busy thinking about their contribution and influence most likely anyway. If anyone is reading or analyzing your work super closely or with scrutiny, most likely they are looking for something they can add to their work, or avoid doing as they produce their work. We are mostly focused on ourselves, and this can be used as leverage to free your mind from concerns about others' judgments. Most people are not going to spend much time thinking about it hence *create for yourself*! As a creative person, it's my job to share. It's my job to create. It's my job to put myself out there in the world creatively, *but it is not much of my business what others do with it.*

We are all natural creators. We are designed to create, to build, to flow, to share our creative gifts with others, whether it be in our relationships, our jobs, our homes, or the natural world around us. We are part of it and thus, we are designed to create. When we take our ego out of the equation, we are free. Just like young children who play and create games and make-believe worlds in an instant without a second thought of judgment or self-criticism that stops them in their tracks, we are here to play. We are playmates at this game of life, and I encourage you to take on that mindset the next time you begin a new creative project. No judgment, just play.

I am setting this chapter free...it is certainly not perfect. *Yet right now that is not my business.* I have sat with these words for months, and it is time to set them free to do their work in the world. I think I corrected all the typos. I believe my grammar is correct. I know for sure that my intention is pure. I am sharing my struggle with perfectionism in this way so that *you* can consider your relationship with it. To possibly change it, if yours needs changing. The world will be much happier with fewer perfectionists and more fulfilled humans in it. If you are one of the perfectionists (and you know who you are), I invite you to *free yourself.* Free yourself from that self-created prison because you are not doing your truest work in that jail, and you are the only one keeping yourself there. It is lovely out here in the free world of creativity, on the playground of life where we can create for the sake of itself, as we are designed to do. *Just for fun* and *the sheer joy of the process of creation.*

This chapter is going to end here. Abruptly. Not perfectly, because well...that is the whole point of my message: I don't have to say it perfectly anymore, I just have to say it. And set it free.

POEMS JUST FOR FUN:

I'm breaking free from the chains that bind me
Setting in my soul and my body free
Leaving those gloomy days behind me
Said goodbye to my misery
Because life is a sweet sensation!
Sacred, precious, and rare
So set your glorious mind to create in kind
And know that you are created to share.

Your gifts *inside you...*
Let your wisdom guide you...
Perfectionism can't find you...
If you no longer hide you...
Set yourself free*!*

HAIKU'S ON PERFECTIONISM:

Perfectionism
Do you play this deadly game?
Killing dreams quickly.

You are not alone.
Many live in this prison
Free yourself, just play.

AN ACROSTIC POEM:

P is for Perfect and we all know its a lie
E is for Everyone who struggles with it at times
R is for Realization that you are not alone
F is for Forge ahead and soon you'll find your zone
E is for Engagement with the passion of your choice
C is for Clarity when it's time to raise your voice
T is for Tomorrow when you get another chance
to own your truth, your perfect truth with this the
*   world enhanced!*

You are perfectly imperfect
You are perfectly aligned
To perfectly imperfectly share
The gifts you've been assigned.

Maybe you're not perfect
That means you're not alone
You are here to share your gifts
Imperfectly...like this poem!

We are all natural creators in our own mediums. We are designed to create, to build, to flow, and to share our creative gifts with others.

— LITA VALLIS

Lita Khatibi Vallis wasn't born in Austin but she got here as quick as she could. After 20+ years here, she considers herself a native by way of Seattle and New Orleans, where she spent 28 years prior to her arrival. She came for the music and stayed for the amazing people and friendships she formed here. Lita sang around town when she first arrived, hitting the open mic scene and grabbing a few gigs here and there.

Her passion for songwriting and singing have been renewed during the cocoon period brought to us all in 2020, by way of COVID-19.

As she shares the story of her ongoing battle with perfectionism, she has also been practicing what she preaches by revisiting her childhood passions, taking online piano and songwriting lessons, and writing and singing every day since March of 2020.

She is a party and event planner and chief Party Priestess at Celebrate To Elevate, the event planning company she co-founded with her bestie (one of her co-authors here as well), Laura Wall. With over 15 years of experience hosting and throwing life-changing parties and celebrations, Lita looks forward to combining her passion for events with her passion for music and creating a new iteration of Celebrate To Elevate which will encompass all her gifts, in 2021. Stay tuned for more, in the meantime, you can follow her on Instagram @LitaVallis and @celebratetoelevate as well as on Facebook at Lita Khatibi Vallis. Hear Lita's original songs on Spotify, Amazon Music, iTunes, or Youtube under Lita Khatibi Vallis.

LAURA WALL

ALL THE BULLIES I'VE LOVED BEFORE

I want women to be free. To be free to express themselves. To be free to control their bodies, their careers, their lives, and who they want to become. I want women to know that they have an inherent power within them, but to be able to fully employ it, they have to protect themselves from bullies.

When I say *bully*, what comes to your mind?

Are you thinking of the mean kid in school who steals kids' lunch money, calls them names, and pushes them down on the playground? It is a prevailing stereotype, but nowadays the bully has left the classroom and grown-up, taking their tactics into adult life. Bullying can happen to anyone at any age with the injuries not only being physical and emotional but mental and spiritual too. The repercussions can affect both the psychological and physical well-being of the victim for years to come, as well as impacting their personal and professional relationships.

I know this to be true as I have had upwards of 50 bullies over my lifetime. Some of you well-meaning readers might be thinking right now: "Well, if you are for women's empowerment, then you need to stop giving your power away."

Great advice. *Except, I never knew I had any power.*

Looking back, I realized that I have been bullied throughout my life since age five. I was bullied by a variety of opponents including friends, family members, boyfriends, employers, and business partners.

I have been called names, given the silent treatment, harassed, blamed, shamed, put down, gossiped about, gaslighted, manipulated, and even physically accosted. All by people I knew. Strangely enough, many of them, I cared for, admired, and even loved.

When I say "bully," I am referring to someone who uses their power, mental faculties, physicality, and/or position to dominate, control, or intimidate someone else. The stupidly seductive part of bullying is: *they make you think that this horrible treatment is all your fault.* Bullying is not just one person dominating the other. It is a dysfunctional dance between two people who are, in a peculiar way, agreeing to play certain roles.

For the aggressor, it is their primary communication style. At some point in their life, they have learned that this behavior gets them what they want. The victim unwittingly accepts this poor treatment. Why? Probably, they may not know any other way to express themselves and because they think they deserve it. Also, the victim believes that their behavior of avoiding conflict, staying still and silent, will perhaps prevent what they don't want: loss, separation, or pain.

Bullying is not just about power, but it is about boundaries. The aggressor is pushing in, and the victim is not resisting.

WHAT I HAVE COME TO REALIZE IS:

1. <u>Everyone</u> is your bully if you don't have any boundaries.

And I didn't have boundaries for a long time.

For much of my life, I did not have healthy boundaries, and in many cases, I had no boundaries at all. My policy was *peace at any price*, which set me up as an easy mark for anyone who wanted their way, was power-hungry, wanted to test their limits, or had a desire to use me as a means to achieve their goals. I agreed when I didn't want to. I absorbed people's comments, unable to respond. I kept the peace at great sacrifice: my mental sanctity, my emotional and physical comfort, and my sovereignty, that is, my ability to govern myself.

2. When we are confronted with intense conflict, we fight, flight, or freeze.

This is natural and normal. It is how our nervous system is wired for survival.

We unconsciously move into these states of being: fight, flight, or freeze.

For many women, freezing may be the most common: do nothing, say nothing, and then move on without ever addressing the grievance. What we may not realize is that our lack of action is only reinforcing the pattern of conflict we wish to avoid.

3. To create an effective boundary, you need a clear plan.

Early on in my life, I had no plan for dealing with bullies. I started to see my repeating pattern of being in relationships with aggressors. I found I was missing the four parts of a good defense: skills, strategy, confidence, and allies.

Since I think we all understand what a physical bully is, I will be sharing my stories of the *other* types of bullies and the insights I gained.

THE STORY OF A, AN EMOTIONAL BULLY

An emotional bully creates chaos and instability by constructing an environment around them where people jump to "fix" the situation.

Many bullies use "head games" as part of their attack, but for **A** that was all she used. As the youngest child in a family that had suffered the loss of another child, my best guess is that **A** found that she could use her emotions to get what she needed from her mother and father. This is what she did for the rest of her life too.

I knew **A** nearly all of my life and had seen a lot of erratic behavior from her. But as I was a child most of the time, I had no idea that this was dysfunctional.

A was my grandmother.

I moved out of my house when I was 17 after diligently saving my money from a part-time job. I had become estranged from my family after an incident in our Christian fundamentalist church. I wasn't so sure about God and needed space from my parents.

My one-bedroom apartment was clean but located in a rough part of town, near the University of Texas where I was attending college. When my grandparents discovered my living conditions, I could tell they were worried and displeased. With little consent on my part, they made plans to move me to a condominium.

The condo was furnished and much nicer than my last place. My grandparents stepped in and took on the role of my parents, coming to visit from time to time, and making sure I was eating well and studying.

I had a serious boyfriend who stayed over quite a bit. I kept this secret from them, as my grandparents were helping pay for the rent, and because they strongly disapproved of him.

Keeping secrets from **A** was the norm for our family. I had been trained at a young age to carefully curate what I told **A** about my daily activities when she and my granddad came for a visit, which was nearly monthly. I had kept the details of my college romance from her, knowing it would only upset her. I worried about how she might react.

At the urgings of my boyfriend, I started counseling sessions, hoping to repair the rift with my parents. The therapy had the unexpected side effect of my seeing the unhealthy dynamics with my grandparents as well.

I loved my grandmother, but I was also afraid of her. She was so good at the "silent treatment" game -- where you were completely ignored indefinitely. She would not speak to you until you figured out what you did wrong and made it up to her. You just never knew what might set **A** off.

I was baffled and strangely empowered at the sight of **A**, who was not silent after I had delivered the news of my college romance.

A's chest heaved uncontrollably as the sobs trickled out in small batches. She was stooped over my kitchen table with her forehead pressing down on her forearms. The cries of a wounded child from a 70-year old woman unsettled me.

Freshly armored with new communication methods from my recent counseling sessions, I had intentionally come to this conversation determined to change the pattern between **A** and I. I was determined to disrupt this odd dance we had participated in since I was a child.

"Don't tell **A** about going to summer camp. Or riding a horse there," said my mom emphatically, in preparation for **A**'s visit to our home when I was nine. This was the first step in my training on how to deal with my grandmother, and how to communicate with her safely. We *had* to keep secrets from her. If we did not, we suffered the wrath of her toxic emotions.

And now those emotions were leaking all over the wooden table in my kitchen; my grandmother was hysterical. My grandfather stood nearby with an ominous scowl on his face and chastised me, "Look at what you have done," gesturing towards **A**. He always backed her play, probably to keep the peace in their marriage. His attempt to shame me didn't work this time.

"Look at what she is doing to herself," I replied, astounded at the words coming out of my mouth. I was standing up for myself.

I had just told them "no," and it was a first for us all. I turned down their demand that I would ditch my boyfriend and friends, and spend the 4th of July weekend with them. I felt like I was being asked to prove that I loved **A** more than my boyfriend. **A** was upset when she found out that I was seeing him, but was even more upset that I was not choosing her. I expected silence so I was not prepared for this double whammy, first from her and then from my grandfather. Their collective response to my attempt to set a boundary felt juvenile and punitive.

"Fine," said **A**, suddenly more calm and focused. She moved into full battle mode, barking orders to my grandfather, "Henry, move the television set. We are taking it back home with us."

She employed the "take your toys and go home" maneuver.

When I first moved into the condo, my grandparents helped me give me an old TV set of theirs for my living room, along with a few other possessions to help "feather my nest" and make my college living space more homey and enjoyable.

They went on to scoop up anything that was "not appreciated" by me and left.

As the door closed behind them, I collapsed into a puddle of tears myself. Wondering how I was ever going to get them back in my life and repair this giant chasm in our relationship.

THE STORY OF F, A MENTAL BULLY

The goal of the mental bully is to remove your feeling of safety. They use mind games of fear, shame, blame, and accusation to create self-doubt and remove your ability to trust yourself. The duality of their behavior (both as the rescuer and the attacker) makes you distrust them and yet, want to prove that you are trustworthy.

Similar to most high school romances, my romance started wonderfully. I was nearly 15 when I met **F**, who was 19. I was pretty enthralled that an older boy was interested in me. With a family inheritance at his fingertips, he courted me like nothing I'd ever seen before. I was pampered, adored, and treated like a queen. Cards and flowers are left at my locker. Dinner dates at upscale restaurants, not the local pizza hangout.

Most of all I loved that he would drive from the other side of town and pick me up for lunch in his expensive car, in front of my friends. I relished his efforts in showing me how much he loved me.

As we started college, his trust fund began to run dry, and he was not able to keep a job. He moved in with me, into my apartment, while I worked three part-time jobs and went to college full-time. Eventually, I grew frustrated with his lack of income and his overbearing attention, and I broke up with him. I moved to the other side of town, hoping to put some physical space between us.

A well-meaning friend thought I needed a new man in my life and set me up on a blind date with **D**, who treated me quite similarly, rolling out the red carpet on our first date, throwing money around, and name-dropping.

After an expensive dinner where **D** detailed all of his professional connections and luxury possessions, he suggested that we watch a movie at his house located in one of Austin's affluent neighborhoods. I agreed, thinking that maybe we would be able to have a more down-to-earth conversation in a private place.

At his house, the movie we were about to watch together turned into "whatever you want to watch on cable" in his living room while he disappeared.

After a little while, I wondered where he had gone and went looking for him. I found him in his room, in bed, with his shirt off, his lower half under the covers. My heartbeat started speeding up inadvertently.

"Oh shit, he is naked!" I thought.

D patted the space on the bed next to him, "We can watch the movie here."

Unprepared for this turn of events, I offered a nervous "Uh, no, thank you. I'll watch the movie in the living room."

Sitting in front of the TV, I stared blankly and waited. Thinking that he would put his clothes on and join me. He didn't.

Timidly I went back again and cautiously peeked around the doorframe of his room and asked "Would you please take me home now?"

"Now?" he replied "Naw, I'm too tired. Why don't you just sleep here and I'll drive you home in the morning?"

Baffled by his reply, I retreated to the living room again, my heart racing like a rabbit facing a wolf. In my panic, I could not think of what to do. I was 19 years old, estranged from my whole family with no close girlfriends that I could ask for help.

After my brain shouted "Danger! Get out of here!" a solution finally came to me: call my old boyfriend, **F**. **F** and I were still friends. I knew that he cared for me and thought I could count on him to help me out of this tricky situation.

After calling **F** from the house phone, I became a bit paranoid. I nervously tiptoed through the house, closing the front door behind me with a delicate touch. **D** was unaware I was leaving. I was afraid **D** would hear me, confront me, *and then what would he do?*

I arranged to meet **F** down the street. Once I was safe in **F's** car, I felt so relieved and tearfully recounted the evening, my mistakes, and my regret. It was now 4:30 am.

As **F** started the engine, he said "let me show you something" as he drove south. Which was strange, since my apartment was located north.

The highway became a country road. **F** turned down a dirt path, partially covered with weeds. It looked like we were on someone's private property, heading through a field with a stand of big oak trees in the distance.

"Where are we going? I said.

F said nothing, his face emotionless. My stomach began to drop out like the downhill slide on a rollercoaster. We kept driving, leaving behind the streetlights and signposts, into the dark, the headlights showing only endless rows of tall reeds.

My nervousness began to build and spill out of my mouth as I whined "**F**, where are we? What are you doing?"

Again, my pleas were met with stony silence. I got that sick feeling like something bad was about to happen, but I was powerless to stop it. It was 1987. I had a small handbag from my night out. I was in a sexy dress with pantyhose and high heels, and no cell phone. In those days, cell phones were the size of a brick and only rich people like **D** had one. I could no longer see any houses or other roads, no way to get help even if I could walk through this unfamiliar terrain.

My mind struggled to make sense of what was happening.

*"**F** wouldn't hurt me. He loved me then, and he still loves me. He came to rescue me and now he is going to..."*

Before I could finish my thought, the car stopped. **F** said "Let's get out and walk a bit. I want to talk to you."

His voice sounded like his old self again, friendly and relaxed.

Breathing a silent sigh of relief, I exited the car, thinking, "That was weird. Maybe I was overreacting."

By now the sky had gone from dark to slightly dusk signaling that sunrise and another day was upon us. I was ready to put my horrible date night behind me.

Once out of the car, I was confused by **F's** body language—his arms crossed over his chest and a slight scowl on his face. I had thought everything was okay, but now my clenched stomach was back. Without any warning, **F** became judge and jury, reviewing my case: my date with **D**.

He asked me lots of probing questions: how I'd met **D**, where we went on our date, what we had done at **D's** house. Despite feeling embarrassed and ashamed, I answered him truthfully, as we had made a promise when we'd dated, to be honest with one another.

He eventually came to the last part of the date about me going to **D's** house and doubting my story, questioning if I had stayed in the living room and not in **D's** bed. By now, I was crying and begging him to believe me. As quickly as he had turned against me, he turned, got in his car, and drove away. Leaving me standing alone in a field.

I screamed and yelled, chasing the car, hollering his name into the cloud of dust kicked up by the tires. I fell to my knees, stickers and small rocks biting into them, and sobbed uncontrollably. I was surrounded by waist-high weeds and silence. My fear was paralyzing. I could not think of what to do but sit there. It was like I was a stunned animal on the side of the road who had been hit by a car. The sun was peeking through the trees at me, a reminder it was about to get hot. It was August. I had to get moving.

I walked a little and cried a little. The tissues from my purse were long spent, so I had to stop occasionally and use the edge of my dress to wipe my face. My high heeled shoes were hurting my feet, but taking them off only promised sharp rocks and stickers instead of blisters.

I kept my eye on the horizon, hoping this semi-visible path would lead me back to a road. Roads meant houses and people…and help.

Not wearing a watch, the time had a way of expanding, allowing me far too much time to think. I used every moment to replay the events on repeat, looking for clues as to why I had gotten here. Which led me to more chest-tightening crying. Before I ever found the end of the path, I heard the sound of a car engine. I wasn't sure what to wish for: that **F** wasn't coming back for me, or that he was.

For a moment, I hoped it would be the property owner…like a kindly grandfather-type in an old beat-up pickup truck. Instead, I saw the glint of sunlight on the hood of a familiar car. **F** was heading my way.

When he pulled the car alongside me, he leaned across to the rolled-down window, and gently said "Go ahead, get in."

Timidly I climbed into the seat, now aware and embarrassed by my streaked mascara and stained dress. I think I held my breath for the whole way back to the main highway. That's when he began to explain what he had done and why. I don't remember much of it as I was still afraid **F** might ditch me again, afraid to trust that he would actually take me home. However, I do remember the gist of it is that he wanted to show me:

…what could have happened when I go off on a date with someone I don't know.

…how naive and stupid I had been, and...

…the potentially dire consequences I might have encountered because of my poor choices.

F insisted that he had created this melodrama "for my own good," so I could "learn my lesson."

F explained, he had done this *because I trusted him so much.*

That's when I put the pieces together and realized he had planned this nightmarish excursion intentionally, probably from the moment he got my panicky call. When he was done talking, I just sat there, letting the hot mascara-filled tears run down my face, ruining my dress even more. I couldn't say anything as I was numb from the shock and shame of it all.

THE STORY OF Z, A SPIRITUAL BULLY

A spiritual bully is someone who uses your very best God-given gifts, such as kindness or compassion, against you.

It started as a blind date with my best friend arranging a connection with **Z** by brokering a barter arrangement: we provided some business services in exchange for both of us having a spot in **Z's** upcoming business marketing course.

Initially, I was thrilled as it seemed like a sweet deal: I was getting a high-priced business course, and the work I was to do was fun and easy for me. Plus, I got to do all of it alongside my best friend.

My excitement was quickly dampened upon meeting **Z** for the first time, replaced by a niggling sensation of doubt. I could not put my finger on why exactly I had a funny feeling. My intuition was giving me a clue to leave, but I stayed.

I went to the group meetings, took notes, listened, and did the business course work.

On the other side of the barter, I worked diligently for **Z** in her business, attending planning meetings, taking notes, and communicating via text and email.

I also attended group networking meetings where **Z** spoke. I was enamored by her passion and drive. Her eloquent speeches were a rallying cry that inspired the crowd to take action. I made friends with many incredible women who attended, as we all seemed to be connected to the message of women supporting women.

As I look back, I realize that my glass-half-full optimism sought out and found the best parts of **Z** and her business offerings. At each of our business meetings with **Z,** I learned of her vision to bring more resources to women in business, to bring in accomplished speakers for business training, as well as her plan to give back to our local community through fundraisers, and the mentorship of young women. I was elated that I had finally found a leader whom I could admire and follow.

As time went on, I began to see not a leader for the collective good, but a recurring pattern of psychological and emotional manipulation that only benefitted **Z**.

My intuitive nudge came back again three months into this arrangement. An email was sent to our business course group. A ping in my stomach told me there was a lie hidden somewhere in the message. A lie that would allow **Z** off the hook for her commitments, while making her look like a victim who was doing their best to keep the business course on track. I was unsure how to address it, and again, I moved forward without taking action.

With my awareness heightened, I began to notice certain behaviors and language patterns when interacting with **Z**.

If I was providing business services to her and set a boundary around a work deadline, she ignored it, would feign ignorance, and then apologize and give emotional excuses that tugged at your heart, playing the victim role.

I would be angry and frustrated but would instead focus on the greater good my work was providing to the women impacted by her business, and swallow my concerns. Silence, dedication, and diligence were my coping mechanisms.

For our business course, we had a major deadline with a celebratory event tied to it. Which seemed to have been forgotten, as **Z** did not adhere to her own boundaries. Again, pleading with our group and playing upon our kindheartedness, **Z** asked for extensions, our understanding, and yet, expressing how hard this had been on her emotionally. The group seemed to willingly ignore the lies, delays, and lack of professionalism.

I held a unique position as I worked both for **Z** as a contractor, and also with **Z** as her client. As I saw the inside workings of her business and spent more time with her, I could see that her focus was scattered and sporadic. Despite a long list of accomplishments, she longed for significance and a true connection with others but did not know how to go about creating it. Many times I truly felt sorry for her and tried to offer friendship and emotional support.

Finally, the ever-escalating volume of my intuitive voice got my attention when our business course group received another misleading communication. I confronted **Z** publicly and became the target for her vitriol. The victim became the bully as **Z** went on the attack.

In the aftermath, I met with several of the women from the business course group who reached out to me and thanked me for standing up to **Z**. They each had their own story of being put down, manipulated, or gaslighted by her. They each shared a hidden desire to speak up but feared "rocking the boat." They acknowledged their complicity, expressed shame, and seem to accept all of the responsibility for the way **Z** had treated them.

I was horrified and edified.

I researched narcissism. A narcissist is a spiritual bully, usually drawn to empaths, who are known for their kindness, heartfelt and peace-loving nature. My educated guess is that our group of women who undertook the business course were mostly empaths.

A narcissist is skilled at using the victim's strengths against them. I realized that our group all shared similar traits of compassion and a strong desire for unity and collaboration. All of these traits had been used to keep us from rebelling against **Z's** tyranny.

A small disclaimer: *I didn't really love all of these bullies. I thought I did. In reality, I had a misplaced sense of loyalty and care for them. I was overly optimistic and hoped that if I were nicer or more compliant they would treat me better.*

Let me be clear, the stories I have included here are about real people in my life. Although I refer to them as bullies, they are not villains. They were all people who were doing their best, based on their patterns and belief systems. They were doing what they thought was right, to get their needs met, to communicate in the way they knew how, and to achieve a particular outcome. Looking back, I am grateful to each of them because they acted as my boot camp of sorts to help me build my boundary-making muscles.

Maybe this is part of your journey too. You've been a doormat in relationships or weren't sure how to speak up for yourself in an awkward situation.

Below are a few lessons I learned and suggestions that may help you get stronger in setting appropriate boundaries so that you receive what you need, and you block what you do not.

STEPS TO CREATING STRONG BOUNDARIES

1) Define. You have to figure out what you want. And sometimes that is gained by learning what you don't want. That is part of the lesson of the bullies: they show you the behaviors, interactions, and thought patterns that you don't want. Once you know what you want, write it down. Having a tangible list of guidelines of your own helps reinforce it in your mind.

2) Train. Our upbringing may or may not have included lessons in the right skills or strategies in dealing with difficult people. Learning the right language style, tone of voice and body positioning takes time. Take a course in communication skills or negotiation. Learn different strategies of communication for different personalities. Then train yourself using these new tools by practicing setting boundaries with a few close and trustworthy people. Your allies will help build you up and can provide valuable feedback and support when you are dealing with a challenging conversation. Training with your allies, having some new tools for conversations and practice will build your confidence.

Warning: *you will need to set your "nice girl" aside and step into your power. Remember, no is a complete sentence, and adults don't always have to explain their reasons.*

3. Reconnect. Our bodies, minds, and hearts are very wise and are designed to give us signals and feedback when something is not right. We all have some form of intuition. Maybe you call it something else...God, Holy Spirit, that little voice, or gut instinct. Reconnect with it and listen to it. It is there to guide our decisions and help protect us from the bullies.

4. Redefine. For those boundary busters and narcissists in your life, you will need to reset your boundaries, taller, wider, and stronger than before. Initially, you may have to build a brick wall where before you had only a chain-link fence, so to speak. Setting bigger, bolder boundaries is a necessary and normal response to constantly having them overridden. You can always adjust them as more trust in the relationship is established.

Most of all, you have to redefine your idea of who you are, and who you want to be. You have to take an active role in choosing to act and react differently, to get skilled in handling conflict differently, and listening and trusting yourself more.

You have to figure out what you want. And sometimes that is gained by learning what you don't want. That is part of the lesson of the bullies: they show you the behaviors, interactions, and thought patterns that you don't want. Once you know what you want, write it down. Having a tangible list of guidelines of your own helps reinforce it in your mind.

— LAURA WALL

Laura Wall is a co-founder of the Hearts of Healing Center (HOHC), a registered 501(c)3 non-profit organization devoted to bringing more love and light to the world through spiritual development, counseling, and holistic healing services.

With 12 years in the health and wellness industry as an entrepreneur, best-selling author, coach, and speaker, she now offers intuitive coaching and mentoring to women who want to show the world their authentic selves and incorporate their spirituality into their business. Laura is passionate about reminding her clients to live out their divine potential: embracing their truth, wielding their superpowers, and chasing their joy.

Laura is also a Healing Guide, offering AromaFreedom, a healing therapy that blends neuroscience, psychology, and aromatherapy to facilitate the release of limiting beliefs and recurring negative emotions.

All services provided through HOHC are given freely in devoted partnership with the abundance of the Universe. Donations are always gratefully accepted and are tax-deductible.

Laura is an engaging leader and an accomplished speaker, teacher, and facilitator who offers presentations on a range of topics including stress-management, productivity, habit building, creativity, spiritual laws, and healing. Please contact her below if you would like her to speak to your group.

When she is not "in captivity" due to COVID-19, you will find her traveling to tropical locations like Costa Rica and pursuing her other passion: surfing.

You can reach her here:

www.heartsofhealingcenter.org

Instagram: @laurawall.tx

Email: laurawall.tx@gmail.com

JENNA ZANTUA

BECOMING DIGITAL AND BOUNDLESS

Pronounced as Halu-Halo, which means "mix-mix," is a popular Filipino frozen dessert made up of a hodgepodge of ingredients you stir, and the result is an uber refreshing snack that's perfect for a hot summer day. While the Halo-Halo may seem to an outsider, a bizarre-looking dessert, for me, it's a beautiful creation sent from dessert heaven.

I'm sorry if I'm making you think about food right now, and swear it's unintentional. I only wanted to share this one dessert that I think represents much of the mixed culture that I grew up with as a Filipino.

The Halo-Halo itself is similar to my country's history, which is a true melting-pot of pre-colonial matriarchal society with Chinese, Malay, and mixed Asian influence marked by a long colonial history with the Spaniards, Americans, and Japanese ways of life and thinking.

As for me, this is the easy Halo-Halo version of me: I'm a bilingual female with a splash of Spanish and a little sprinkle of Russian (more on this later). I speak and sound like an American (not that I do it on purpose). Also, a significant portion of my native language is Spanish. I look somewhat a mix of Pacific Islander meets Southeast Asian and most days I like to cook Asian food, but nothing beats the taste of home when I eat adobo or sinigang (with rice.)

I am truly a distinct blend of culture and tradition, yet it's good that as a Filipina, I can adapt and relate to many types of people. It has been a constant battle to find my true identity as a woman of color living on the other side of the world from where I grew up.

THE BIG MOVE

Probably my biggest life decision was moving abroad with my family over four years ago. My husband, who is an international school teacher suddenly got a job offer to teach in Russia. I was a restaurant business owner and on the side, I was doing HR consulting with corporate clients.

I thought to myself: *Am I ready to make this big move?* I was a new mom who had just given birth to my daughter when this opportunity came. And to make things even more complicated, we had just purchased a house a few weeks before all of this happened.

Was I scared? Definitely. *Did I think about what could happen to us, and all the possible outcomes?* Hell yes. Yet, it was one of those rare moments where I just knew it deep in your bones: it was the right thing for us to do as a family. I just felt how our lives would change drastically the moment we left. It was a gigantic leap, a new, exciting, and scary adventure, so to speak.

For the next two years of our life abroad, I devoted myself to the art of becoming the best and most outstanding stay-at-home mom ever. I learned how to cook many cuisines, mostly both Russian and Cyrillic. I learned how to operate the washing machine (just for context; it was always the laundry shop that did our clothes so this was something new to me) and clean the apartment (not my favorite thing to do). I was also breastfeeding and taking care of our baby. Life was busy and it was cold all year long.

Then, just like that, two years had passed by, and it was time to move on to another country, Panama, a place much farther away, yet quickly became our new home. I adapted to the pace of living in a new city, settled into our new apartment, found out where the park was, the grocery store, a new coffee place, and enrolled in Spanish class. Also, I found a nice local daycare where my daughter could easily learn Spanish and be with other kids.

On my daughter's first day in school, I found myself at home with nothing to do, and then suddenly, I realized for the first time, I could go back to working full time. Things were changing and it was time for an alternative plan. I am grateful for being able to have an ex-pat lifestyle where moving from one country to another is normal. I had become acclimated to things changing, and no longer feared the thought of adapting, yet instead, I welcomed it. However, there's always my frenemy, *fear*. The friend who was constantly whispering the cautions, the what-ifs, and the doubts in my ear.

Where do I find the courage to forge my path? How do I even begin? All I knew then was I had a strong desire to find my new identity and a new endeavor that would light up and awaken my sleeping entrepreneurial spirit.

CHANGE IS INEVITABLE

Zero. That's what I had to start with when I went back to work full time after two years of being a stay at home mom. I remember the thoughts vividly, the ones that were running inside my head: *Can I really do this? Do I still know how to communicate at this level? What can I offer that people will buy? Where do I even begin? What do I have to do to make this work?* Breathe. I told myself. Just breathe. And when I did breathe, I realized that *the beauty of zero is starting from a clean slate.*

Reinventing myself and learning all the things I have always wanted to learn didn't seem so bad after all. I am a dreamer and have always wanted to do big things. I wanted to create an impact on the lives of others, no not like the Mother Teresa or the Bill Gates kind of way. I just wanted to make sure that I was contributing a little something to the world and to do this, I knew I needed to widen my network. Thank you for the infinite possibilities that the internet offers, and this book project which is headed by Allison Ramsey, founder of Empire Life, and Empire Life. Thank you to all the authors featured here in this book too, for all your support. While the internet is both a blessing and a curse for humanity, it was more so a tool that enabled me to connect with amazing people, and ones I would never imagine meeting in this lifetime. In the online world, I felt borderless and limitless hence I planned my next move just like I always had planned things, I started with a big vision, a pen, and a good ole notebook.

MY INSTAGRAM SHOP AND THE $5 OFFER

I was sort of a newbie in the online space, back in 2011, and I joined Odesk (now Upwork) as a freelance SEO article writer because why not do that. I loved writing, and I heard people were making money online. I was still holding a corporate job and was curious about the online space. My first gig was to write five articles and was paid $24.44 for 5 articles. I jumped for joy even though it was just a teeny tiny amount in payment for the work I did. *Why?* This proved to me that not everyone on the internet was a scammer.

It didn't take long for me to take on more writing gigs. I was a ghost-blogger for a popular nail salon in the US (what a super fun gig), and then I became the ghostwriter for a CEO of an HR-related SaaS company. Also, I wrote numerous product descriptions for e-commerce sites, furthermore, all of the gigs I did were not enough to sustain a decent living for me to be able to leave my corporate job. I still wasn't able to crack the code on how to earn a sustainable income online. At that time, I decided this was going to be *just a hobby* because my writing gigs were inconsistent until I became a full-fledged direct response copywriter in 2018.

I was a multi-passionate entrepreneur and this ran in blood and through my veins. Then I started hearing about selling on Instagram, immediately, I set up my account, learned the ropes, and quickly grew my account to 2,000 active followers who are my ideal clients. I sold bags, lipsticks, shoes, and anything trendy for women at that time. My merchandise was always sold out, but because I was not the manufacturer of these items, I didn't get to enjoy a huge profit margin. It was such a thrill to be able to sell online to strangers, but because it was not my only bread and butter, I didn't do anything more to take my online store to the next level.

Fast forward to 2018, I was now ready to try the online space yet again, but this time as a service provider. After all, I had nothing to lose because I was coming from a long hiatus from work and transitioning from being a stay-at-home mom to a work-from-home mom. I updated my profile and reached out to my network of friends who are working online for support. A good friend of mine, who was a successful online entrepreneur veteran, referred me to her US-based client who was looking for an extra pair of hands. I did the interview, easily got an offer and the conversation went like this:

Caucasian, male client: So Jenna, I think you'll be happy with the offer of $5/hr.

Me: Well, not really... I live in an expensive city and that is way too low.

Caucasian, male client: It's more than what most people earn in your country.

Me: I know that, but I don't live there so our expenses are different. Thank you for the offer but it's not enough for me.

It was a short conversation, but one that I would never forget. If I lived in my home country where the cost of living is lower, I would probably think about it but I was raised by parents who believed that I am capable of having much more. At this point, I just knew I would be miserable working for someone who saw me only for my color and not for my worth. Yes, he probably didn't mean to offend or insult me, but the fact that he thought I was only deserving to be paid a certain amount because of where I came from is already fundamentally wrong in many ways.

Soon after, I got hired as a headhunter for clients in the US and the UK but because the work wasn't steady enough, I looked for another job and got hired to be a project manager and copywriter for a sales funnel agency. It was my entry into the agency life where I learned many things about marketing and online operations. Many people say your time working online seems to go by faster than in a regular job because of its fast-paced nature, and I felt this to be true when I starting. Everything felt urgent and there was always a client launching a new product, course, or service. True enough, the lifespan of holding a job online seems shorter in duration possibly, my guess is because a lot of people are hustling and that includes me. I needed to find other clients to support and increase my income. Through my consistent desire to increase and add to my income, I became an operations manager for a digital consulting agency. I hired people and helped grow this agency. My learning was accelerated once more from doing projects and client management and in everything from sales, operations, and fulfillment. Unbeknown to me at that time, these were all the essential components that would help me realize that I could build my own business and make it on my own as my own boss.

REDEFINING THE HUSTLE

Before I get to the part about becoming my own boss, let's talk about the online hustle and how I used to have no boundaries. While I enjoyed this time learning everything about the online space, I wasn't prepared for the long hours or clients who thought they owned my time. In short, I had zero boundaries when it came to working. I was grateful to have the opportunity to work from home and to be working again but I didn't realize that it would take such a toll on me physically, mentally, and emotionally. I was working 14 hours days and sometimes even more hours than this. I allowed clients to have the ability to reach out to me any time of the day and even on weekends. I replied to clients even when I wasn't supposed to and I worked on weekends and didn't take a day off until I was at the point of crashing and burning.

By having no boundaries, I opened myself up to abuse, and an ex-client used to call me up on Sundays just to talk about his personal woes, and I allowed him to do this because I didn't want to lose my job. My scarcity mindset, at the time, was telling me that I might not be able to get another good-paying job like this and I allowed all of this to happen even with knowing I had a toddler and a husband constantly waiting for me to finish up so I could be with them fully.

I thought I could do it all because I was *just* working from home and thought I had all the time, in the world, to accommodate tasks and requests from clients. Boy was I wrong and I was hustling hard *just* to make it. I had my eyes on an income goal and forgot about my why and who I was doing all these things for. I knew I needed to get out of this bad cycle, I prayed and mustered enough courage to leave clients (and a steady flow of income) who were not in alignment with my values and my new goals. I sought professional help to process all that had happened to me, I used to beat myself up over the fact that I was the only one responsible for everything that happened to me. Over time, I also learned how to make peace with life events by setting strong personal and work boundaries. I now have a hard rule of not working on weekends unless it is something that truly lights me up or if it's a worthy cause. Part of my learning process was also investing in my personal and professional growth for me to be able to turn my online freelancing career into a full-fledged service-based company.

I became a certified Director of Operations and a certified online business manager. I hired a lifestyle business coach, and I joined a group coaching program to uplevel my business as well as network with more female founders. As I write this, I am still in the process of learning and discovering new things and meeting new people online. I am constantly redefining, as the title of our book, the way I work to fit my intended lifestyle, and that involves more time with family and creating impact.

MY ENTREPRENEURIAL JOURNEY

I always wanted to become a lawyer, but after graduating from college I realized that I was tired of doing school work. I wanted a real-life experience and all the benefits that came with it. Then like most typical young adults, corporate was the way for me to go and was the closest to the "money", at least it seemed like it.

Yet, in my heart, I was always entrepreneurial and business ideas were welcome at the dinner table. I come from a family of entrepreneurs, from my Lolo (grandfather), my Lola (grandmother), my aunt, my dad, and my two brothers. We were all about building businesses in my family.

At 10-years old I remember my earliest recollection of entrepreneurship, was selling stationery and pens to my classmates. On the weekends, I would go with my aunt to Chinatown in Manila and this meant waking up early as it was at least a two-hour trip. Tita (aunt) Juliet gave me a small capital and I used this to buy the goods to sell for the week. I don't remember what I did with my earnings at the time, most likely I bought loads of junk food. Every summer my siblings and I would be selling halo-halo outside our house and I am pretty sure we ate most of what we were selling. It was one of my earliest experiences in selling and knowing the cost of goods and profit margins were. In corporate, I would even sell second handbags and clothes just for the heck of it.

At 22 years old, I opened a small food kiosk even when my money was tight. It was a hit and we had a lot of people wait in line for hours just to get our food. You would think it would be successful but because I didn't know anything about operations or finance, it became a failed venture quickly. I was devastated, and I questioned my abilities and then went back to corporate accepting that I still had a lot to learn. For the next five years, I would push out the consistent calling of starting my own business. I always had ideas that I could never fully implement because I was working for someone else.

In 2009, I had the idea of opening a nail spa in my hometown then I quickly went to work and put up a plan. I worked on the branding, attended training, and hiring people. After a year, I sold the business to my business partner because I could not give my time to fully supporting the business while still holding a corporate job. The location of the spa was also an issue, and the market wasn't ready for what we had to offer. This was another huge blow to my self-esteem and another failed venture that didn't last.

Sometime in 2011, I made a big decision to go back to my hometown to join the family restaurant business. This meant a huge pay cut and I learned everything there is to know about operations and human resources. Even though I was pulling in 12-hour shifts, it didn't feel like it was a lot of work because I loved every single minute of what I was doing. Two years later, we opened a bakeshop, and while the products were really good, the location was not quite right and I didn't know how to do marketing. I closed the bakeshop soon after to cut our losses. This was followed by one closure after another of the branches that didn't do well. I had gotten used to opening and closing businesses so much that it no longer affected my disposition, instead, I looked at every closure as an opportunity to learn and be better next time.

GOING DIGITAL AND BOUNDLESS

Now if you do not know me, I have always been a planner or at least I'd like to think I have control over things and life. When you're multi-passionate like me and want to do ten million different things, planning is key but plans always change. I know this, you know this, and we probably all know this.

The year 2020 though had other plans, it was as if the pandemic took hold of my google calendar and erased all of my plans. All my plans went: *Poof. Gone, and just like that.*

The year 2020 was a constant reminder of how many circumstances can change in a heartbeat. It seems a lifetime ago and yet it was just over four years ago when we made our way to Russia, our first country as ex-pats. We did this trip with four enormous suitcases, a newborn baby in tow, big dreams, a dash of hope, and a sprinkle of fear.

Once the pandemic happened I became committed to my growth and personal self-development. I invested in certifications, coaches, and even bought online courses. I was determined to do better in dealing with my boundaries and to have enough focus on things that mattered to me. When I first started in the online space three years ago, I wasn't aware of pricing, rates, and what it meant to be a person of color in this space. Specifically as a woman of color working in the online space. I wasn't aware until I started meeting other women who were also doing the same thing but were getting paid twice or thrice as much as I was making. When I hit my first five-figure month, I thought: *This is it, I'm right where I want to be.* I exceeded my revenue goal without feeling like I was always chasing or hustling. I never imagined I would one day be in a growth environment and surrounded by women who uplift other women. The online space gave me a sisterhood of strong women who are successful in their chosen fields and are truly supportive of one another especially with this book REDEFINE, and the incredible co-authors you will read here too.

It was for this reason that I decided to work and support female founders through tech and visibility. I have a vision of helping thousands of female entrepreneurs in setting up their technical needs, and visibility components of their online businesses. Why? Well, these two important components of an online business are often the two main reasons why women are not able to move forward with their businesses online. I want to be their ally and the person who can implement and make things happen for them.

STEPPING INTO MY POWER

Today, I have a roster of amazing female entrepreneurs on my team and that I support. These women never questioned my rates and my capabilities. They didn't see me as a woman of color, they saw me as someone fully capable of helping them with their businesses. By learning how to SAY NO to things that do not serve me and my clients, I can open up more space for opportunities to work only with people who respect my values. Throughout this journey, I learned a lot about myself. I would never be able to discover these had I not taken the plunge into going full time in my online business. If you have a dream or an idea you've been sitting on for ages, I feel the first step is commitment. Commit to doing consistent and conscious actions every day because taking one step is better than not moving forward at all.

Be fearless.

Be bold.

Be boundless because you are.

My scarcity mindset, at the time, was telling me that I might not be able to get another good-paying job like this and I allowed all of this to happen even with knowing I had a toddler and a husband constantly waiting for me to finish up so I could be with them fully.

— JENNA ZANTUA

Jenna Zantua is a digital ex-pat living in Panama. She is an online business strategist and consultant that helps women founders with brand positioning, strategy to build, systematize, and maintain profitable online businesses.

She is a certified director of Operations, certified online business manager, brand copywriter, digital marketing geek, amazing cook, tough mama of one, fiercely loyal friend, and wife to Steve Aoki's (better-looking) doppelganger...

Also, she is a badass female entrepreneur and founder of Digital & Boundless™, an online company that provides top-notch strategic tech and visibility implementation support for impact-driven small businesses. Digital and Boundless™ utilizes technology, automation, systems, and processes that help women entrepreneurs grow their online business with ease and less overwhelm.

She hopes to see more women-owned businesses grow and thrive in the big, exciting, vast, and sometimes scary, and online universe.

Laura Wall Co-Authored Book - "Finding Our Wings: Seven Entrepreneurs on Reclaiming Hope and Power."

Lita Vallis Co-Authored Book - "Women Entrepreneurs Volume I: We Are Brave: 14 Inspiring Stories: Women Entrepreneurs Who Conquered Fear, Self-Doubt & Adversity to Build the Business of Their Dreams."

ACKNOWLEDGMENTS

OPEN LETTER FROM THE CO-AUTHORS TO ALLISON RAMSEY:

As a guide in this journey, we admire Allison's courage. We believe it comes directly from her intuition which makes her an engaging leader for us as well as we follow our intuition. We know she is on her path, leading with love and a true desire for each of us to have our best outcome. This book has been an inspiring journey and Allison has played a significant role in that inspiration.

I WANT TO THANK:

My Daughter, the best treasure, best friend, and consistent inspiration. The best most celebrated choice I have ever made to become a mom. I am thankful for you every day. I feel you are my guide *just* as much as I am yours. It is a gift to see the person you are and are becoming. I am grateful to have this opportunity to be your mom and appreciate all of our moments together. Thank you for being my biggest supporter and there for me.

My Mom, a constant strength and guide in my life, and a great friend. I thank you for your honesty, your integrity, your grit, and your stamina in gracefully guiding my strong willfulness growing up. Thank you also for being the absolute best Grandma we can wish for. Thank you for your patience in listening to your two super strong-willed children make their cases in everything to you, sometimes for days. Thank you for coming to all my sports games and events. Thank you for your continued support with this book and encouragement, and support in my business.

My Dad, you worked endlessly for our family, your work ethic has been passed down for generations, how you are always generous with your loved ones, you want everyone to be having a good time, you let me have my own ideas, teaching me how to box, teaching and guiding me in understanding girls are strong, girls are fierce, girls are strong leaders, and always fully accepting me for exactly who I am, thank you for being constant in my life of a great friend and strong leader. Thank you for understanding me even often before I understood myself and still giving me grace. Thank you for often coaching my sports teams, coming to all my sports games, events, and your continued support of this book, and my business. Thank you for being the DJ at my first business event.

My Brother, I am proud of you, thankful for growing up with you watching out for me. Thank you for giving me the chance to have continuous open discussions with you growing up, in those I learned to make my case, do solid research, have an understanding of what I was pointing out, and if and when I was successful in making my point to you I knew it was a valid point. This strengthened my negotiation skills later in life, this strengthened my resolution to make my case and gain respect, friends, and have the influence needed. Always being able to talk to you about anything. Thank you for being the best player at Monopoly most likely anyone will ever meet, for all times we played Monopoly, those showed me a lot of strategies to take into life.

My Grandparents, all now passed away. Thank you for watching over me always, thank you for your continued display of hard work ethic when you were alive and with us. Thank you to my dad's parents for displaying to be a long-lasting marriage. Thank you to my dad's mother for her strong fiery spirit. Thank you to my mom's mother for her dedication to her family. Thank you to my mom's parents for displaying to me a long-lasting marriage. Thank you to my mom's father for being the patriarch of his family and how much he enjoyed bringing everyone together.

All my Aunts and Uncles.

All my cousins and their children.

My best friends, Christina, Mabi, Meagan, and Jessica.

All my Family.

My previous bosses, who truly mentored me.

My Mentors.

My Coaches.

All the Co-Authors, their loved ones, their mentors, their families, their best friends, their coaches.

My team of experts at Empire Life.

The two Editors of this book.

My Formatter of this book, Michelle Morrow.

Everyone who has ever believed in me and gave me positive accolades of encouragement along this path. I heard every word and it means something to me. Thank you.

All of my online communities, my Facebook Group, my Instagram, my LinkedIn, my Twitter, my Facebook, all of you mean the world to us at Empire Life. We hear all your comments and highly appreciate your support.

My board of directors I am on at my University, thank you for your continued support.

To my University, you all displayed to me what community was all about in being away from family and living in a new city while in college, I am truly grateful for my experience there.

My previous professors.

My team lead at the University I teach courses and am a Professor at. For your continued support and belief in me.

The teachers who believed in me.

My previous principals, who did not call my parents when I was sent to their office! You have no idea how grateful I am for this, and for you listening to my consistent negotiation skills.

For those school principals, I had who saw my leadership, grit, and worked with me. I'm truly grateful for you solidifying my leadership capabilities. When you supported my ideas I understood and carried through my life the philosophy related to grit in seeing clearly, 'There is always a way.'

My ancestors worked hard for us all to be here, in all their struggles, in all their successes to bring us here to this point in time.

My ancestors, who have passed and continue to inspire us with their legacies.

To all my sports coaches growing up, you gave me a thick skin, you gave me the chance multiple times to be the team captain and devote myself to my team. You gave me the opportunity to lead spirited teenagers to our state championship wins. You showed me how to research a team, make a strategy, and clearly plot success for our team. I carry these strategies over often into managing and scaling my company. Thank you for instilling in us how being on your team was more than a team it was a family and we watched out for each other.

Thank you to my College Swim Team Coach, you had a solid, stern, supportive presence when speaking. Thank you for displaying your leadership to our team and for your patience with all of us.

Thank you to everyone who made this book happen and all of your support in supporting us in being best selling authors.

www.ingramcontent.com/pod-product-compliance
Lightning Source LLC
Chambersburg PA
CBHW061248120726

48001CB00001B/204